WHY DID THIS HAPPEN?

by Bob Yandian

20 19 18 17   10 9 8 7 6 5 4 3 2 1

Why Did This Happen?
Copyright © Bob Yandian

ISBN: 978-168031-141-9

Published by Harrison House Publishers
Tulsa, OK 74145
www.harrisonhouse.com

TABLE OF CONTENTS

Chapter 1: Tragedy 1
What Is Different About a Tragedy?
Does God Answer Prayers?
A Season of Mourning Is Permitted

Chapter 2: David and Bathsheba 5
Geographically Out of God's Will
Another Layer of Sin
Uriah the Patriot
Let's Try Again
Only One Thing Left to Do
Ministers Often Get the Worst Jobs
The Long-Term Effects of Carnality
The Death of the Newborn Child

Chapter 3: How to Handle a Tragedy 19
Eight Things David Did to Recover from His Tragedy
It's Time to Get Up and Get Back to Life

Chapter 4: Satan's Greatest Trap 31
God Always Brings the Answers
A City Set on a Hill

That Which Is Hidden Will be Revealed
Times and Seasons
Don't Run from God
Wait on God
Patience, an Indicator of Maturity
Don't Cast Away Your Confidence

Chapter 5: Trust What You Know 47
Agreeing in Prayer
Paul and Silas
Paul and Silas Prayed and Sang Praises
John the Baptist
Elijah in the Cave
When the Bible Is Silent
Don't Compare Yourself to Others
What About Job?

Chapter 6: What About James? 65
Peter Delivered from Prison
Reasons for Unanswered Prayer
Stephen Stoned
Paul's Stoning

Chapter 7: Seed Never Fails. 77
Casting Down Imaginations
The Fiery Furnace
Daniel and the Lion's Den
The Seed Remains the Same
The Word Remains the Same
The Message Remains the Same
The Woman at the Well
Habakkuk and the Fig Trees

FOREWORD

I watched a debate one evening on television between a leading Christian minister and an atheist. The atheist was asked what event in the life caused him to no longer believe in God. He said he was raised in a church and his parents were strong Christians. The dramatic change occurred when his father was dying. He prayed to God for his father to live, but he died. From that time on he no longer believed in God. He said that most of the leading atheists came from the same kind of background. When trusting a supposed loving God ended in disappointment, they turned against God and no longer believed in His existence. They became strong voices in the scientific world for people to turn from the myth of God and follow rational empiricism.

This sounds extreme to many Christians. They would never think of turning against God because of a disappointment. Yet, when faced with unexplainable circumstances, when God seemed unloving and uncaring, they quit going to church. They stopped witnessing to others about Jesus and basically disengaged from any spiritual life at all. They may not have become an atheist, but they are no longer proud to call Jesus their Savior.

The Bible is filled with stories, some ending in great triumph, and others ending in seeming disappointment. In most cases, the Bible gives us the story behind the story and we can understand why many ended the way they did. Yet, in life, we are not always aware of the story behind the story. Why didn't we get the answer we desired? We think we did everything right, yet, God seemingly let us down and His word did not work.

I heard a message many years ago from a Christian business leader, Bob Harrison, who spoke at a minister's conference. He gave the story of how David pulled out of a tragedy. I never forgot the message, but left it in my notes for many years. Then I finally pulled it out one day and made it into my own sermon. That sermon, along with many others from the word of God have made up the basis for this book. How do you handle circumstances which seemingly make no sense? The subject of this book is how to recover from tragedy or confusion over God's reaction to your situation.

I trust you will see yourself in the teachings of these pages and reinstate your trust in the God Who promised to deliver you from all afflictions, and cause all things to work together for your good. Even if you have disappointed God, He will not let you down. Let's get up and begin moving again. There is a wonderful life for you to rejoin.

Pastor Bob Yandian

1

TRAGEDY

Both the Old and New Testament remind us that we believers will encounter afflictions at some point in our lives. Jesus said that we would go through tribulations and trials, but He also promised to bring us through them.

> Many are the afflictions of the righteous, but the Lord delivers him out of them all.
>
> *Psalm 34:19*

In fact, we encounter so many afflictions that we have to be reminded of the specific ones we have been delivered from. That's why I believe it is important for us to make a daily journal of answered prayers and miracles God has brought to us out of our times of trouble. This helps us to remember all His benefits (Psalm 103:2).

WHY DID THIS HAPPEN

WHAT IS DIFFERENT ABOUT A TRAGEDY?

What makes a tragedy different than a trial, affliction or persecution? First of all, a tragedy makes no sense to the natural or spiritual mind. Knowing where to begin to pray when a tragedy strikes is a major problem for most people. And once the tragedy is over, it can never be forgotten. One reason it cannot be forgotten is because it never was really over—it just ended.

No one has to remind us of the time we came through a tragedy. We think about it automatically without a prompting or reminder. For instance, what if your mate divorced you after you had prayed for the marriage to work out or for them to come back one day? If that doesn't happen, you may begin to question if there is something wrong with you. You will think, *Was it my fault? I prayed but seemingly have not gotten an answer.*

I believe the worst tragedy of all has to be the death of a child. When you experience the loss of a child, your world is instantly turned upside down. Children should not die before their parents. In fact, any parent would gladly trade his or her life for their child's.

After a barrage of prayers from parents, brothers, sisters, relatives, friends and a church full of faithful and concerned believers, what do you do if your child dies anyway? Unfortunately, when this happens, many people tend to leave the church and stop living for the Lord because their prayers were seemingly not answered. They reason that if God did not answer these prayers and heal the child, especially if the child came from a wonderful family with believing parents, then why should they think that God would answer any of their prayers.

DOES GOD REALLY ANSWER PRAYERS?

Of course, He does! In some cases, however, He doesn't answer them exactly like we think He should or exactly how we thought He would. When this happens, we think that what we have trusted in for years does not work and that God, in some way, has failed us.

Many people just can't seem to move on after a tragedy. They get stuck at a point and even years after the event is over, they get up in the morning and rehearse the story throughout the day until they go to bed at night. When they meet someone and begin a conversation, they retell the same story, reliving the tragedy all over again while hoping to find some closure.

These people exited the ride of life ten or fifteen years ago and cannot move on. They do not want to assume the responsibilities of life. They think that it would be easier to close the bedroom door, stay in bed and pull the covers over their head. They want an explanation before they move on. They say, "If God would just explain to me what happened, I could begin to live my life again." But God is waiting for them to begin moving again in faith, then He will explain it to them.

A SEASON OF MOURNING IS PERMITTED

Weeping may endure for a night, but joy comes in the morning.

Psalm 30:5

Mourning is permitted by God; it is scriptural. Israel was told to stop and mourn the death of Moses for forty days. Then they were divinely commanded to get up and move on again. Many probably reminded God that He had told them Moses would take them into the Promised Land, yet now they were following someone new— Joshua.

In 1 Samuel chapter 10, God told Samuel to anoint Saul as the first king of Israel. But later, God told Samuel that He was through with Saul and was going to appoint a new king. Samuel tried to change God's mind and begged God to give Saul another chance, but God told Samuel, "How long will you mourn for Saul, seeing I have rejected him" (1 Samuel 16:1).

Finally, Samuel obeyed the Lord and was sent by God to the house of Jesse to anoint David as the next king. David ended up being the best king Israel ever had. He set the standard for all kings after him. Even Jesus came to sit on the throne of His father David.

Tragedy is not a stop sign. When we experience a tragedy in our lives, we should yield—slow down or even stop temporarily. We can use this time to get reoriented and then begin to move again.

2

DAVID AND BATHSHEBA

For the believer, any trial or tragedy has an end. After the clouds part, the sun will come out again. Let's take a look at the story behind David's tragedy to see how he recovered from the death of his newborn son.

This story, like any other event or tragedy, had a beginning. David's story of unexplainable problems and later recovery began in 2 Samuel Chapter 11.

GEOGRAPHICALLY OUT OF GOD'S WILL

This chapter in David's life started in the spring of the year at the time when kings go out to battle. David was supposed to go to Rabbah and fight with his troops but instead, he decided to stay home and send his commander, Joab, out with the troops. David was geographically out of God's will. He probably had a reasonable excuse. Maybe he wanted to pray, study his Bible or write a psalm. Yet, he did none of those things.

And it came to pass, after the year was expired, at the time when kings go forth to battle, that David sent Joab, and his servants with him, and all Israel; and they destroyed the children of Ammon, and besieged Rabbah. But David tarried still at Jerusalem.

And it came to pass in an eveningtide, that David arose from off his bed, and walked upon the roof of the king's house: and from the roof he saw a woman washing herself; and the woman was very beautiful to look upon.

2 Samuel 11:1-2, KJV

Notice, David got out of bed in the evening. Evening is the time you go to bed, not the time you get out of bed. He had probably been watching *Days of Our Lives, Jeopardy* or an old movie, and then went to bed. David was bored. All his friends were at battle—where he was supposed to be.

David should have recognized his problem, asked God to forgive him, jumped on his horse and gone off to battle, and this tragedy would never have happened. But instead, he walked out on the patio of his palace and saw a beautiful woman bathing. If the Bible says a woman is beautiful, you can count on it. Bathsheba was gorgeous! You might be asking why she would bathe outside where she could be seen. Well, for one thing, all the men were supposed to be out to battle, including her husband, and the few men who were left in town were guarding the gates of the city. Bathsheba did not know that King David was at home.

ANOTHER LAYER OF SIN

No sin ever begins large. Sin begins small and almost insignificant. Jesus told us that adultery does not begin with the act itself, but rather with the unrepentant thought and meditation of sex (Matthew 5:27,28). With only the thought, you have plenty of time to repent and never suffer the consequences of a fulfilled action. Instead of repenting at this point, however, David had Bathsheba brought to his palace bedroom and had sex with her.

> And David sent and enquired after the woman. And one said, Is not this Bathsheba, the daughter of Eliam, the wife of Uriah the Hittite?
>
> And David sent messengers, and took her; and she came in unto him, and he lay with her; for she was purified from her uncleanness: and she returned unto her house.
>
> *2 Samuel 11:3-4, KJV*

Bathsheba was ripe for getting pregnant, and that's exactly what happened. After a few weeks, she contacted the king and told him she was going to have his child. David was faced with another layer of sin and personal problems brought on by his own self-centeredness.

> And the woman conceived, and sent and told David, and said, I am with child.
>
> *2 Samuel 11:5, KJV*

But again, David did not repent. He instead tried to cover his sin through his own effort.

> And David sent to Joab, saying, Send me Uriah the Hittite. And Joab sent Uriah to David.
>
> *2 Samuel 11:6, KJV*

David brought Uriah, Bathsheba's husband, home and tried to get him to go to bed with his wife. David figured that if Uriah slept with Bathsheba, the child would be seen as his and David would be free. David did not care about Bathsheba at all. She would have to live all her life with a lie and a child she knew did not belong to her husband. She would have to carry the regret alone for the rest of her life.

URIAH THE PATRIOT

At this point, David became a hypocrite. Just like any carnal believer, David wore a thin veneer of spirituality but was filled with selfishness and fleshly plans. He was scrambling for a plan to cover his sin and decided to bring Uriah home to a heroes' dinner, in order to get him to sleep with his wife.

> And when Uriah was come unto him, David demanded of him how Joab did, and how the people did, and how the war prospered.

And David said to Uriah, Go down to thy house, and wash thy feet. And Uriah departed out of the king's house, and there followed him a mess of meat from the king.

2 Samuel 11:7-8, KJV

Uriah probably wondered what was going on as he sat at the king's table and feasted on the finest meal he had ever eaten. He had been taken from battle and brought home by the king's command, leaving his military brothers to fight the battle without him. All he probably thought about was the necessity of getting back to the battle. What could the king be thinking by removing him from such a crucial conflict? Any accolades could be given when the war was over. Why now?

With all the hypocrisy David could muster, he told Uriah what a great man of battle he was and that he deserved a little R and R. He not only gave him a great meal, but also a box full of the finest food to take home to his family.

David probably watched with great anticipation as Uriah left his house. Uriah, however, did not go home but instead stayed at the gate with the soldiers who guarded the city. If he could not be in battle, he would get as close to military duty as possible. Don't you know that the guards must have thanked Uriah for the meal that night?

But Uriah slept at the door of the king's house with all the servants of his lord, and went not down to his house.

2 Samuel 11:9, KJV

When David found out the next day what Uriah had done the night before, he could hardly believe it! He asked Uriah why he did not go home to his family. Uriah's answer should have shaken David to his very core. He told David, "The ark, and Israel, and Judah, abide in tents; and my lord Joab, and the servants of my lord, are encamped in the open fields; shall I then go into mine house, to eat and to drink, and to lie with my wife? as thou livest, and as thy soul liveth, I will not do this thing" (2 Samuel 11:11, KJV).

What a patriot! What a loyal servant Uriah was to David and Israel even though he was a Hittite, not a Jew. Uriah and his family were believers in the Lord of Israel, calling Him "my Lord," and had sworn their allegiance to the God of Abraham and the nation divinely given to him and his descendants. David should have been cut to the heart for his own sin and disregard for such a wonderful family. He should have immediately asked God for forgiveness and informed Uriah of his sin with Bathsheba.

LET'S TRY AGAIN

David tried to get Uriah to go home to his wife, Bathsheba, one more time. This time, however, David decided to get Uriah drunk. David thought that perhaps Uriah would stumble home after losing control of his faculties. Of course, Uriah might pass out on the doorstep of his house, but if he was drunk enough, he would not know if he slept with his wife so Bathsheba could say he did and the child would be seen as hers and Uriah's. If the plan worked, no one except Bathsheba and David would know the truth.

But as drunk as Uriah was that night, he once again stumbled to the guard house and slept with the soldiers who were watching over the main gate of the city.

And when David had called him, he did eat and drink before him; and he made him drunk: and at even he went out to lie on his bed with the servants of his lord, but went not down to his house.

2 Samuel 11:13, KJV

ONLY ONE THING LEFT TO DO

David had only one more option as he continued with his plans to cover his sins. He had to murder Uriah. David wrote an order to be given to Joab, who was commanding the troops at Rabbah. The order was given to Uriah for delivery, which meant he delivered his own death sentence to his military leader. Joab was told to command the troops to advance on a city wall, but then retreat as soon as they met resistance. Everyone was to know the command except Uriah, who would be left alone in the forefront of the hottest battle.

And it came to pass in the morning, that David wrote a letter to Joab, and sent it by the hand of Uriah.

And he wrote in the letter, saying, Set ye Uriah in the forefront of the hottest battle, and retire ye from him, that he may be smitten, and die.

And it came to pass, when Joab observed the city, that he assigned Uriah unto a place where he knew that valiant men were.

And the men of the city went out, and fought with Joab: and there fell some of the people of the servants of David; and Uriah the Hittite died also.

2 Samuel 11:12-14, KJV

Uriah was such a faithful soldier, he never even looked at the death letter he carried. Uriah was not killed by the enemy in battle; he was murdered by David, his king and spiritual leader. After the news of Uriah's death, David brought Bathsheba into his own home to be his wife.

David looked like a hero to the nation of Israel as he brought the pregnant wife of a war hero into his own home, promising to take care of her for the rest of her life. David had turned the whole incident into a political opportunity to win favor with the citizens who looked to him as their spiritual and natural leader.

At the news of Uriah's death, Bathsheba mourned for her husband. Despite her sin, she loved her husband and carried half the blame for his death. Sin always affects innocent people, especially those in your own family.

Earlier I said that only David and Bathsheba knew what had happened, but the end of the chapter tells us that someone else knew and was unhappy with what David had done—the Lord.

But if ye will not do so, behold, ye have sinned against the Lord: and be sure your sin will find you out.

Numbers 32:23, KJV

MINISTERS OFTEN GET THE WORST JOBS

It looked like David had escaped what could have been a scandal, until God told the whole story to a minister, Nathan the prophet.

> And the LORD sent Nathan unto David. And he came unto him, and said unto him, There were two men in one city; the one rich, and the other poor.
>
> The rich man had exceeding many flocks and herds:
>
> But the poor man had nothing, save one little ewe lamb, which he had bought and nourished up: and it grew up together with him, and with his children; it did eat of his own meat, and drank of his own cup, and lay in his bosom, and was unto him as a daughter.
>
> And there came a traveller unto the rich man, and he spared to take of his own flock and of his own herd, to dress for the wayfaring man that was come unto him; but took the poor man's lamb, and dressed it for the man that was come to him.
>
> And David's anger was greatly kindled against the man; and he said to Nathan, As the LORD liveth, the man that hath done this thing shall surely die:

And he shall restore the lamb fourfold, because he did this thing, and because he had no pity.

And Nathan said to David, Thou art the man. Thus saith the LORD God of Israel, I anointed thee king over Israel, and I delivered thee out of the hand of Saul;

And I gave thee thy master's house, and thy master's wives into thy bosom, and gave thee the house of Israel and of Judah; and if that had been too little, I would moreover have given unto thee such and such things.

Wherefore hast thou despised the commandment of the LORD, to do evil in his sight? thou hast killed Uriah the Hittite with the sword, and hast taken his wife to be thy wife, and hast slain him with the sword of the children of Ammon.

Now therefore the sword shall never depart from thine house; because thou hast despised me, and hast taken the wife of Uriah the Hittite to be thy wife.

Thus saith the LORD, Behold, I will raise up evil against thee out of thine own house, and I will take thy wives before thine eyes, and give them unto thy neighbour, and he shall lie with thy wives in the sight of this sun.

For thou didst it secretly: but I will do this thing before all Israel, and before the sun.

2 Samuel 12:1-12, KJV

I'm sure Nathan did not want to confront the king with what he had done. As king, David could have had Nathan killed. Yet, throughout the Old and New Testament, ministers have had the unpleasant duty of confronting national leaders with their sins. So how could Nathan call himself a prophet and not correct the king?

Nathan presented the whole story to David as a parable (paraphrased):

A poor man had a pet lamb that was loved by the whole family. A rich man lived across the road who had many sheep. A visitor came by the house of the rich man and stayed for dinner. Instead of killing one of his own sheep, he went across the road and took the pet lamb of the poor family and killed it for his guest.

When David heard this story, he was incensed that someone in his kingdom would commit such a selfish act. Yet, the story was about him!

THE LONG-TERM EFFECTS OF CARNALITY

By this time, David had been out of fellowship with God for almost a year so his spiritual perception was dulled to the point that he could not pick up on the simple meaning of Nathan's story. He had regressed to the place where he needed to learn the first principles of the oracles of God all over again. David had regressed to the point of a spiritual child.

For when for the time ye ought to be teachers, ye have need that one teach you again which be the first principles of the oracles of God; and are become such as have need of milk, and not of strong meat.

Hebrews 5:12, KJV

In his anger, David shouted out that whoever had done this would pay fourfold. Nathan then proceeded to tell David that he was the man in the story. He had gotten Bathsheba pregnant and murdered her husband. David—and David alone—was held accountable by God.

The moment David heard God's voice through Nathan, he confessed his sins and said, "I have sinned against the Lord" (2 Samuel 12:13, KJV). Nathan's next statement is incredible, "The Lord also hath put away thy sin; you shalt not die" (2 Samuel 12:13, KJV).

A whole year's worth of sins was forgiven in one instant! Oh, the grace of God toward David, and toward us.

If we confess our sins, He is faithful and just to forgive us our sins and to cleanse us from all unrighteousness.

1 John 1:9

Nathan's second statement astonished me even more when he said, "You will not die." David had committed two capital crimes under the law—adultery and murder—yet was not going to face the death penalty. I know God's grace is great, but I am going to have to ask God when I get to heaven: "Why did You choose to forgive David, even to the farthest extent of the law?" David deserved to die, and yet was pardoned by God. I have a hard time wrapping my mind around the greatness of that statement.

> Howbeit, because by this deed thou hast given great occasion to the enemies of the Lord to blaspheme, the child also that is born unto thee shall surely die.
>
> *2 Samuel 12:14, KJV*

Nathan told David that the child born to him and Bathsheba would die. Notice that David had opened the door to Satan, but God would not allow the curse to go outside David's family. The fourfold curse would come to pass, but it would not touch the people of Jerusalem and Israel because they were innocent.

David said that whoever had done this would pay fourfold. David had opened up his family to four things that would occur. David's four problems were spoken out of his own mouth.

1. David's son died.
2. One of David's sons lusted for his sister and raped her, committing incest.
3. Absalom found out about the incident and murdered his own brother for raping his sister.
4. Absalom died in rebellion, trying to overthrow his father's kingdom.

David rode out all four of these things and went on to be the best king Israel ever had. He left a legacy for all the kings after him to follow. Each subsequent king was judged as a success or failure based on whether or not they followed in the footsteps of their father, King David.

THE DEATH OF THE NEWBORN CHILD

David thought perhaps God would be gracious toward the child as He had been with his sin, but despite David's prayers and fasting, the child died. This was David's first tragedy. How he handled this tragedy became an example of how we too can handle something we do not understand, something that upends our faith and leaves us wondering about God's love for us. Like David, a great life awaits us if we correctly handle the tragedies of life.

3

HOW TO HANDLE A TRAGEDY

When a tragedy occurs, we have to choose how to handle it. David had to choose how to respond when his child died. He was operating under an assumption that God might be gracious and let his son live, even though Nathan told him the child would die. David thought that if God forgave him and said that he would not die, perhaps his son could also live. Of course, this did not happen.

David's recovery from this tragedy is the subject of the remainder of 2 Samuel chapter 12. His story becomes our example.

Then David arose from the ground, washed and anointed himself, and changed his clothes; and he went into the house of the Lord and worshiped. Then he went to his own house; and when he requested, they set food before him, and he ate. Then his servants said to him, "What is this that you have done? You fasted and wept for the child while he was alive, but when the child died, you arose and ate food."

And he said, "While the child was alive, I fasted and wept; for I said, 'Who can tell whether the LORD will be gracious to me, that the child may live?' But now he is dead, why should I fast? Can I bring him back again? I shall go to him, but he shall not return to me."

Then David comforted Bathsheba his wife, and went in to her and lay with her. So she bore a son, and he called his name Solomon. Now the Lord loved him.

2 Samuel 12:20-24

One of the greatest tests of life is learning to recover or bounce back after a tragedy. Experience is not what happens to you; experience is how you choose to react to what happens to you. After the death of his child, David probably did not want to recover. He probably would have preferred to remain self-centered, to forget everyone, blame God, feel sorry for himself and remain shut off from his family, friends, and responsibilities. But he did not.

EIGHT THINGS DAVID DID TO RECOVER FROM HIS TRAGEDY

The first lesson David learned from this tragedy was not to give in to his problems. He learned to press into them. He did eight things that we can use as examples for us to follow today.

1. He arose. You can't spend your time on your knees because your prayer was not answered as you thought it should be. Just as with the nation of Israel at the death of Moses, there comes a time to move on. David was on his knees before God for seven days. David had already confessed his sins to God when he went to the Lord to intercede for the life of his child. Now it was time to get up and move on with life.

There comes a time to stop praying, hoping to twist God's arm to get what you want. David had to realize that things were not going to change. He had no one to blame for the child's death but himself. David had confessed his sins and had been forgiven by God, now David needed to get up and forgive himself.

There is a certain amount of self-righteousness attached to not forgiving yourself. Continuing to beat yourself up is often a form of false humility. It almost sounds good to say, "I know God has forgiven me, but I just can't forgive myself." Yet, this is the height of arrogance. Who are you to not forgive yourself, when God has forgiven you? Are you bigger than God?

Sin in the Christian life does not make us forfeit the race; it only temporarily sidelines us. According to Hebrews 12, once we are forgiven, we are to get back in the race.

Wherefore lift up the hands which hang down, and the feeble knees; And make straight paths for your feet, lest that which is lame be turned out of the way; but let it rather be healed.

Hebrews 12:12-13, KJV

This is often what we look like after we are forgiven. We feel sorry for ourselves and criticize ourselves. Our hands hang down at our side and our knees are weak. But God is simply telling us to forgive ourselves, lift up our hands, strengthen our knees, and begin to run again!

2. He washed. How you look affects what you think of yourself and what others think of you. In order to turn your life around, you first have to turn yourself around. You can think clearer after you bathe, clean up your life, straighten up your office, throw off your dirty clothes and put on some clean ones. Bathing washes off the dirt from yesterday, just like repentance washes away sin. When David took a shower, he probably watched the dirt run down the drain and was reminded of the grace of God that simply says, "If we confess our sins, he is faithful and just to forgive us our sins, and to cleanse us from all unrighteousness" (1 John 1:9, KJV).

3. He anointed himself. This is not talking about anointing with oil, but rather cologne—fragrant oil—after shaving. Bathing affected what David thought about himself. But shaving and putting on cologne, that was to impact his appearance to others. David was going to show the world it was time to move on. Even though David was confused about the death of his child and God's plan from this point on, he realized life needed to go on.

4. He changed his clothes. David took off his grieving clothes and put on his daily living clothes. He dressed for life again. There was a season change from grieving to getting back to life. When he was grieving, he probably did not care how he looked; but with a change of attitude came a change of clothing. This part of David's story is echoed in the life of Joseph as he came from the dungeon.

> Then Pharaoh sent and called Joseph, and they brought him hastily out of the dungeon: and he shaved himself, and changed his raiment, and came in unto Pharaoh.
>
> *Genesis 41:14, KJV*

Joseph perceived that if Pharaoh called for him to come from prison, he was never going to return there again. He, therefore, threw away his old prison clothes and dressed for life.

Life is a collection of seasons. Defeated people try to hang on to a season after it is over, but victorious people know when a season has passed and move on. Winners take the memories of the old season with them, while embracing the new season they are coming into. When summer is here, it's time to take off the overcoat!

5. He came into the house of the Lord. David worshipped. Though he had pleaded for something from God and seemingly got nothing, David still gave something to God. He gave God his time, his worship and his tithes. David did not run from church when tragedy hit; he ran to church. In fact, he went to church first, before he even sat down with his family to eat and fellowship. Church remained at the center of David's life, even though it seemed like God had let him down.

I have been given the same testimony by people in my congregation about what they miss the most when they are away on their summer vacations. In one particular instance, a family vacationed in a city where there was a church the family had heard about from friends, Christian television and magazines. They were excited to go to that church but once in the service, they were underwhelmed by the praise and worship they had heard so much about and the preaching they were told was so good. When they returned home, they told me they could not wait to get back to their home church.

One couple told me they missed many things about their home and work when they were away, but they missed their church the most. I believe this is how David felt when he wrote Psalm 84. He was living in a tent and the war had gone on longer than he ever imagined it would. He missed his wife, his home and his children, but he missed the courts of worship and ministry of the Word of God most of all. This was the place he wanted to raise his children—on the altar of God's presence.

> How lovely is Your tabernacle, O LORD of hosts! My soul longs, yes, even faints for the courts of the LORD... Even the sparrow has found a home, and the swallow a nest for herself, where she may lay her young - even Your altars, O LORD of hosts.
>
> *Psalm 84:1-3*

At this time of the tragic loss of his son, David offered a true sacrifice of praise to God. Against all feelings, he was saying, "I don't know what has happened, but You are still God and You have not changed. Eventually I may know what happened, but until then, who else can I turn to?"

In times of tragedy, we need to be like David and worship God when we don't know or understand what is going on.

Circumstances change, but God never changes! He is the same yesterday, today and forever (Hebrews 13:8).

6. He came to his own house. Family and friends were part of David's stability and security. When you come through a crisis, you need to surround yourself with those who love you. God does not need you—you need Him! Friends need you and you need friends.

David had to come back to those who were still alive. In mourning for the dead, he could not isolate himself from the living, especially those in his family. Like David, we must take responsibility for family who remain in our trust. The moment a person passes on to be with the Lord, they are out of our hands and in God's hands. David's child was now in God's hands, and God could do a much better job than David in taking care of him. Yet, David's family, servants, military and nation were still his responsibility.

7. David ate. People going through times of grief and loss usually don't have an appetite.

David fasted and prayed for seven days. When he finally did eat, his meal signified finality. It was a sign that his grieving had ended and life goes on. The meal marked the end of fasting and the beginning of a new phase of life.

The meal must have been a great time of celebration because David's servants asked why he was now eating after the passing of the child. It almost looked like David was celebrating the death of his son. But David was letting all who asked know that he was celebrating the future, not the past. Now that the child was gone, it was time to re-enter life. Now was the time to eat and celebrate with the living. Life was not over.

> And he said, "While the child was alive, I fasted and wept; for I said, 'Who can tell *whether* the Lord will be gracious to me, that the child may live?' But now he is dead; why should I fast? Can I bring him back again? I shall go to him, but he shall not return to me."
>
> *2 Samuel 12:22-23*

Notice that David said, "I will go to him, but he will not return to me." David had many questions but in this time of uncertainty, he returned to what was absolutely known. Those who die in the Lord go to be in the Lord's presence. Also, all who are redeemed will see their loved ones and friends one day. Those who die will not come back to join us, but those who are alive on earth will one day go to be with those who have died.

Stability in an unstable situation is only maintained by coming back to what is absolutely known. Many heroes in the Bible faced unknown situations and had to come back to foundational doctrines. For example, Job, in the midst of desertion by friends and seemingly by God, declared, "I know that my Redeemer lives, and He shall stand at last on the earth" (Job 19:25).

In a time when fellow ministers had deserted him, Paul shouted out his belief in God's unchanging and eternal commitment to never leave or forsake him: "I know whom I have believed and am persuaded that He is able to keep what I have committed to Him until that Day" (2 Timothy 1:12). Paul was simply saying that he was saved by his will, but after that, he was kept throughout eternity by God's will.

When situations look impossible and circumstances seem to be overwhelming, we too can cry out, "I know that all things work together for good to them that love God and are the called according to His purpose. I may be confused about many things, but I am sure that God will turn this situation around for my good. God's love and care for me cannot change."

Circumstances do not change God or His Word, but His love and Word can change circumstances. Don't throw away what you know because of what you don't know.

8. David made love to his wife and had another child, Solomon. Bathsheba needed David more than anyone else at that time. All the problems she and David experienced were just as much her fault as they were David's. When David called her to the castle, she could have said no. She could have gone back home when he invited her into his bedroom. Adultery is never one-sided.

Bathsheba had to handle the guilt of her affair with David and the sorrow of losing her husband. She loved Uriah and wept over his death. She had been taken into a home and even though it was the royal palace, it was not her home or her family. She now lived around strangers and the only link she had to her true identity, the child she'd carried, was lost.

David spent a week after the child's birth praying and fasting. When David rose up, he did everything else first. He cleaned up, shaved, went to the house of God, came home and ate a meal with his own children and servants. Bathsheba was the last person he saw. Yet, David knew what he was doing. He must have put his arms around Bathsheba and told her of his sorrow for what he had done to her life. He must have reassured her of his love for her as he continued to hold her in his arms. He then made love to her and she conceived another child.

> Then David comforted his wife, Bathsheba, and went in to her and lay with her, and she bore a son, and he called his name Solomon. And the LORD loved him.
>
> *2 Samuel 12:24, ESV*

Their new son was named Solomon and he lived. Out of disaster came a great blessing. David and Bathsheba conceived the wisest man ever born on earth, next to Jesus himself. Jesus affirmed this in Matthew 12:42:

> The queen of the South will rise up in the judgment with this generation and condemn it, for she came from the ends of the earth to hear the wisdom of Solomon; and indeed a greater than Solomon *is* here.

IT'S TIME TO GET UP AND GET BACK TO LIFE

If David had remained on his knees waiting for answers before moving on, he would not have seen this great blessing. Until you repent and get back to trusting God, you will never see the greater blessing just ahead. To quote a great spiritual source, the movie *Shawshank Redemption:* "You can either get busy living or get busy dying." The choice is yours.

You stand in a long line with men and women of the Bible who, like David, had to make a decision to continue moving with God, despite times of uncertainty. God's plan for your life will not fail if you get up and begin moving again. God has not brought you this far to abandon you. What has always worked in your life will continue to work. Don't throw away what you know because of what you don't know!

The remainder of this book is dedicated to answering the question of God's periods of silence. What do we do if God is not speaking to us? What if we are in trouble and God does not seem to care? How can we go on if God will not give us answers?

WHY DID THIS HAPPEN

4

SATAN'S GREATEST TRAP

Then He taught them many things by parables, and said to them in His teaching:

"Listen! Behold, a sower went out to sow. And it happened, as he sowed, that some seed fell by the wayside; and the birds of the air came and devoured it. Some fell on stony ground, where it did not have much earth; and immediately it sprang up because it had no depth of earth. But when the sun was up it was scorched, and because it had no root it withered away. And some seed fell among thorns; and the thorns grew up and choked it, and it yielded no crop. But other seed fell on good ground and yielded a crop that sprang up, increased and produced: some thirtyfold, some sixty, and some a hundred."

And He said to them, "He who has ears to hear, let him hear!"

Mark 4:2-9

There are four different types of ground mentioned in the parable of the sower: hard ground, stony ground, thorny ground, and good ground. Each type of ground represents the heart of a believer. Hard ground is representative of the believer who hears the Word being taught but rejects it. Then Satan comes immediately to steal the Word from his heart. Stony ground is representative of the believer who hears the Word and receives it quickly, but gives up when trials and persecution come. He does not have enough soil or depth of heart for the Word to produce a good root, so he becomes offended. Thorny ground is representative of the believer who receives the Word and holds on for a while but when prosperity manifests, other things become more important than the Word and the Word is choked out. Good ground is representative of the believer who holds on to the Word and endures all persecution and begins to increasingly produce for the kingdom of God—thirty, sixty and finally one hundredfold. He is a mature Christian.

Often the focus of this familiar parable is the different ways that Satan steals from the immature Christian. Satan, however, also has tactics that he uses against mature believers. For instance, I have met people who have been faithfully walking in the things of God for several years. They were faithful to their church home and have grown in the Word of God yet, when something happens that seemingly contradicts the Word of God, they cannot understand or explain why it happened.

GOD ALWAYS BRINGS THE ANSWERS

Also He said to them, "Is a lamp brought to be put under a basket or under a bed? Is it not to be set on a lampstand?

For there is nothing hidden which will not be revealed, nor has anything been kept secret but that it should come to light. If anyone has ears to hear, let him hear."

Mark 4:21-23

This parable is referring to believers who suddenly put their lamp under a bushel or a bed. The lamp represents our witness, our good works, our conversations about God, and how we live our lives before others. Believers who hide their light are like those who suddenly become self-conscious about their stand for God. They become filled with confusion and doubt. Soon, they don't want people to know that they are even a Christian or that they attend church and believe the Word of God. They are embarrassed to let others know that they believe in divine healing and that God fills His children with the Holy Spirit. In other words, they back off from the teachings found in the Bible, especially when those teachings are challenged by the world. This usually happens because something happened to them personally or to someone they know or someone who is in a ministry leadership role, that they could not understand or explain.

It is true that things happen that we cannot explain. But with God, there is no such thing as a question that has no answer. This parable says there is nothing hidden to our understanding that God will not reveal, nothing kept in secret that He will not bring to light.

Loretta and I were raised in church. When I went to work for Kenneth Hagin Ministries, we knew some things about the Word of God but not much about prosperity. As we began to have a better understanding of the simple principles of trusting God for finances, we made the decision to pay off all our debts, with the exception of the mortgage on our house.

In addition to working for the ministry, I also had a side business duplicating teachings for Full Gospel Businessmen and other ministries in town. During this time, I was asked to do a major conference for Full Gospel Businessmen—both duplicating and selling their messages. Loretta and I agreed together that I would clear $10,000 at this conference, because that is what we needed to get out of debt. We found scriptures, stood on the Word of God, held hands and agreed in prayer. We thanked God and praised Him for what I was going to clear from that day on.

It seemed we had done everything right but when the meeting was over, I only cleared between three and four thousand dollars. Loretta and I began to question, *Maybe this faith stuff doesn't work?* We began to doubt and have confusion, but thankfully we didn't quit God and we didn't quit church. We didn't stop believing the message and we didn't quit ministering. We continued to trust God. Along the way, we learned that the *steps* (plural) of a good man are ordered of the Lord. Yet here we were, trying to get there in one giant step!

There have been some situations where God eventually brought the answers to things I didn't understand. But today, I still don't have answers to all my questions. In the church I pastor, people have died whom I didn't think should have died. I had questions: *God, didn't we do everything right? We prayed. We stood on Your promises. We praised and thanked You. We don't understand.*

Oftentimes, we don't know what is in another person's heart. For instance, once there was a woman in our church for whom we prayed, but she died. I did the funeral and it was one of the most difficult funerals I have ever done because she was so young. It wasn't until many months later, while talking to another woman from the church, that I understood why she died prematurely.

This lady said, "You know, I stayed with her while she was battling against the disease. When you would come to visit, she would say she wanted to live and was trusting God, but she only said those things so she wouldn't hurt you because you were her pastor. Others would come as well, but as soon as everyone left, she would say she couldn't wait to see Jesus. She just wanted to go to heaven." Well, my question about this woman's premature death was answered, but it didn't come over night.

A CITY SET ON A HILL

Jesus is the light of the world, but since He is now seated at the right hand of the Father, we are the light of the world in the earth. Jesus said that a city set on a hill cannot be hidden; it is set on a hill for all to see.

You are the light of the world. A city that is set on a hill cannot be hidden. Nor do they light a lamp and put it under a basket, but on a lampstand, and it gives light to all who are in the house. Let your light so shine before men, that they may see your good works and glorify your Father in heaven.

Matthew 5:14-17

In the ancient world, people knew the value of building a city on a hill. It was more difficult for the enemy to ride uphill to conquer them. The inhabitants of a city on a hill could also more easily see when an enemy was approaching, which gave them time to prepare to defend against the attack.

A lamp in a house is placed on a high place to shine down light on all who are in the room. Lights are placed in the ceiling of our churches so we can read our Bibles and see one another. We don't put lights under the chairs or under the platform of the church because the room wouldn't be illuminated as well if they were there. What am I saying? Let me put this as simply as possible: Just because you may doubt God, that doesn't mean you're no longer a Christian. Your lamp is still lit—it's just hidden. If you don't let the world know about the light on the inside of you, that does not stop you from being a Christian. You are just hiding your testimony because the "light" is your testimony.

Perhaps you once told others about Jesus, talked to them about the goodness of God, testified about how Jesus healed your body and provided finances and then suddenly, something happened that you didn't understand and you have become timid, embarrassed, or even ashamed of the Lord Jesus Christ. This is putting your lamp under a bushel—and Jesus told us not to do that!

THAT WHICH IS HIDDEN WILL BE REVEALED

Sometimes we blame the sovereignty of God when we don't understand the outcome of a certain situation. We think, *Well, maybe scriptures don't always work. Maybe God is sovereign, and sometimes He just lets these things happen.* We take on the attitude that whatever is going to be will be and that God is going to do whatever He wants to do. We feel like we have no control.

> For there is nothing hidden which will not be revealed, nor has anything been kept secret but that it should come to light.
>
> *Mark 4:22*

Don't misunderstand. I believe in the sovereignty of God, but God is not sovereign when it comes to answers. He has promised us that He *will* give us an answer, yet He is sovereign concerning the *timing* of His answer. In other words, God is saying, "Hang in there! I will explain it."

TIMES AND SEASONS

Before Jesus left this earth, the disciples were quibbling about what they would be doing in the kingdom. They wanted to know *when* His kingdom was coming. Yet, Jesus simply responded, "It's not up to you to know the times or the seasons, which are in God's hands" (paraphrased). God promised He will answer us; He just didn't say it would be today. We have to wait on Him and eventually, He will give us an answer.

> And He said to them, "It is not for you to know times or seasons which the Father has put in His own authority."
>
> *Acts 1:7*

Loretta and I have friends whose son died prematurely and it caused them to re-examine their Christian life. Many have found themselves confronted with similar situations and it is in the face of these types of disappointments that we must ask ourselves how determined we are to believe the Word of God and profess our faith in Him.

And *whatever* you ask in My name, that I will do, that the Father may be glorified in the Son. If you ask *anything* in My name, I will do it.

John 14:13-14, emphasis added

Jesus said "whatever" and "anything." He promised He will answer, but He didn't promise the *whatever* and *anything* will be granted in our timing. God wants to answer at the right time—and He knows the right time better than we do.

There are times I have doubted. There are times I have felt threatened. There are times I have been confused. *Yet, I refuse to give in!* I am determined to continue following God because He promised in due time, He will let me know the answers to my questions.

I once did a funeral for a father whose young daughter had been trusting God that her father would not die. She had read books about healing, had healing scriptures laid out, and prayed over her father that he would live and not die. But her father died anyway.

As I ministered at the funeral, I felt impressed that God wanted me to focus on this young girl because she was doubting whether or not He was real or His Word was true, and she was considering not returning to church because she had done everything right, yet her father still died. I looked at her and said, "I want you to understand what often looks complicated to us is simple when God gives us the answer. I'm going to trust God that He will answer your questions and reveal why your father died."

I continued, "You may not receive the answer in this life; it may be when you get to heaven. But God will have the answer. You're young enough to live another forty years on this earth and wouldn't it be sad to run from God for the next forty years and then stand before Him one day after He has explained why your father died and you respond, 'That's it?! I ran from God for forty years because of that?'"

DON'T RUN FROM GOD

God's answers are not complicated; they're simple. I am exhorting you, DON'T RUN FROM GOD! Run *to* God during those times when things happen that you don't understand. You may be confused, but God has promised that nothing hidden will remain hidden; it will become manifest. There's nothing kept secret that God will not reveal.

Our emotions can lead us astray. I learned a long time ago to never make a decision when I'm confused—NEVER! If you are confused in an area of your life, don't do anything. Many times in the midst of confusion, our first temptation is to run.

You may be wondering if I've ever been tempted to run and the answer is "yes." There have been times I've doubted God's Word for a brief moment, but I made the decision to keep pressing through. I refused to turn my back on His Word. Why? Because, as I said before, it's never good to make a decision in the midst of confusion. God is not the author of confusion. Confusion comes from the enemy and God is greater than the enemy. He will answer.

So the question is not *if* God will answer; the question is *when* will He answer? The *when* is where His sovereignty lies. God has told us the times and seasons are in His hands and we are not to question Him about this. We are to just keep following Him.

WAIT ON GOD

Wait on the LORD; Be of good courage, and He shall strengthen your heart; Wait, I say, on the LORD!

Psalm 27:14

Wait on the LORD, and keep (guard) His way, and He shall exalt you to inherit the land; When the wicked are cut off, you shall see it.

Psalm 37:34, explanation added

These two verses give us the key to living the Christian life when we don't understand what is happening in our lives—wait on the Lord. Notice, waiting strengthens us. Yet often, all we care about are answers. God is more interested in our maturity than in providing us with the answers.

Waiting produces maturity. In other words, if the answer doesn't come today, by the end of the day we'll be a little more mature than we were yesterday. If it doesn't come tomorrow morning, we'll be more mature tomorrow night than we were that morning. One of these days the answer will come and when it does, we will be able to handle the answer. Every day we wait, we become more mature in the things of God. And every day we become more mature, God is able to entrust us with more prosperity in every area of our lives including health, relationships, and finances.

If you wait on the Lord and keep His way, *He* will exalt you. Waiting on the Lord will also allow us to see the destruction of those who brought evil into our lives. Of course, we pray for these to find Jesus, but if they don't, God promised we will outlast them and one day we will actually witness their destruction.

> Do not say, "I will repay evil"; wait for the Lord, and He will deliver you.
>
> *Proverbs 20:22, ESV*

God said that vengeance belongs to Him and He will repay. It is not up to you or me to get even; it is up to us to keep following God and trusting Him. It is up to us to continue maturing. One day, God will answer us. In the meantime, it is not up to us to do God's job.

PATIENCE, AN INDICATOR OF MATURITY

Patience is a great indicator of maturity. All of us have experienced times of pressure and endurance. Things have happened that we cannot explain and do not understand. This verse is telling us to handle those times with patience. Patience is a virtue found in mature believers.

> As for that in the good soil, they are those who, hearing the word, hold it fast in an honest and good heart, and bear fruit with patience.
>
> *Luke 8:15, ESV*

> And beside this, giving all diligence, add to your faith virtue (moral excellence); and to virtue knowledge; and to knowledge temperance (self-control); and to temperance patience; and to patience godliness; and to godliness brotherly kindness; and to brotherly kindness charity (love).
>
> *2 Peter 1:5-7, KJV, explanation added*

People often ask for patience, but how does patience come? Romans 5 provides the answer.

> And not only that, but we also glory (rejoice) in tribulations, knowing that tribulation produces perseverance (patience); and perseverance, character; and character, hope.
>
> *Romans 5:3-4, explanation added*

What are we supposed to do in tribulation? Rejoice! Patience will *work* experience and experience is a testimony. It is something you can tell others about. When you are in a trial, rather than crying and saying, "Lord, when is this going to be over? When am

I going to be delivered from this situation," why don't you take the attitude that you are building a testimony? Think about how testifying about how God delivered you from your trial will put a damper on the devil's attempt to bring discouragement and defeat. I can guarantee you are not the only person being confronted by the problem you are facing. There are hundreds of thousands experiencing the same trial, and God will see to it that one day you will cross the paths of some of those people to testify about what God did to bring you through.

DON'T CAST AWAY YOUR CONFIDENCE

Where does confidence come from and what is confidence based upon? Experience. Since God has come through so many times in my life, I have confidence in Him.

Therefore do not cast away your confidence, which has great reward. For you have need of endurance, so that after you have done the will of God, you may receive the promise.

Hebrews 10:35-36

Many Christians cast away their confidence. This passage says not to cast that confidence away for something momentary. In other words, don't throw away your testimony for some momentary thing you cannot explain. Don't allow Satan to whisper in your ear that everything you have believed has been wrong. Don't throw away what you do know for some sudden state of *I don't know what to do.* In other words, don't throw away what you do know for what you don't know.

Cast not away your confidence, because God has been so wonderful and faithful through the years. Don't believe the lies of the enemy that say God doesn't exist or God can't help you and doesn't care, when in reality, He does care.

For you have need of endurance (patience), so that after you have done the will of God, you may receive the promise.

Hebrews 10:36

This scripture doesn't mention how long after you have done the will of God that you will receive the promise, but it says you *will* receive it! It also doesn't say if you're questioning God about something you don't understand, that He is obligated to answer you immediately. It simply states that He *will* answer. The God we serve says there is nothing hidden that shall not be revealed and nothing kept secret that will not be brought to the light (Mark 4:22).

I believe there are many who have had something happen in their lives that seems contrary to the Word of God. There are individuals who believed God's Word and expected to see it come to pass but it didn't, so they have been confused. Yes, they may still be attending church, but there is a lingering question mark, "Lord, what happened?" It could be that their finances haven't manifested the way they thought. Or their question could be in the area of healing. Perhaps it centers around the death of a loved one. Maybe someone lost a child, a father, a mother, someone who was young at the time, and they have not understood why this happened. Maybe someone has been praying for one of their children to come to Jesus, but it seems like things have only gotten worse.

If you are in one of these situations or know someone who is and have begun to doubt God and His Word, if you are ready to hide your light under a basket, ashamed to let people know you're a Christian, I exhort you to hang on! Don't give up! God has an answer.

Prayer:

Father, I thank You as we wait on You, we will grow in You and become strong in You. While we are waiting, we are going to continue to prosper and be blessed and when the answer comes, all glory will be given to You. Father, we thank You right now for the answers that will come for children, loved ones, healing, finances, jobs, whatever the need may be. Father, we simply hang onto Your promise and claim it. Nothing is kept secret that You will not bring it to light, in Jesus' Name. **Amen.**

WHY DID THIS HAPPEN

5

TRUST WHAT YOU KNOW

> Therefore I say to *you*, whatever things *you* ask when *you*
> pray, believe that *you* receive them, and *you* will have them.
>
> *Mark 11:24, emphasis added*

It is interesting to note that the word "*you*" appears five times in this verse of scripture. Notice also that this passage doesn't say "whatever things you ask when you pray for **him** or **her**." Did you catch that? Whatever **you** desire when **you** pray, believe **you** receive them and **you** shall have them. This is a prayer for **you**.

When I am praying for myself, I know when I am in faith and I know if the attitude of my heart is right. But when I pray for others, unless the Spirit of God reveals it to me, I do not know whether the person is actually in faith, nor do I know the true condition of his heart.

Often we become upset after we have prayed in faith for someone and either see no change at all, or the circumstances seem to

WHY DID THIS HAPPEN

become worse. We think to ourselves, *We have prayed in faith, therefore this life should be changed because of our prayer.* But often the problem is that we cannot change another person's life; they must *want* their life to be changed. We cannot control others through prayer. Prayer is not witchcraft. The truth is that not even God can change a person's will. If He could, the whole world would be saved!

According to Mark 11:24, the only person who can be assured of receiving results from your prayers is you. Confusion in the Christian life comes when we pray for someone else and nothing seems to happen—the person we have prayed for doesn't seem to get healed or a child seems to turn further from God. We get upset because we think, *I prayed scripturally. I stood on the Word of God. I believed I received.* We go through a list of things we have done on behalf of another, but it still comes back to this: *You are not accountable for someone else; you are accountable for you.*

AGREEING IN PRAYER

Again I say to you that if two of you agree on earth concerning anything that they ask, it will be done for them by My Father in heaven.

Matthew 18:19

The word "agree" is the Greek word *sumphoneo*. The English word "symphony" is derived from this word. It describes a harmonizing together. However, even with the prayer of agreement, you can only be certain whether or not you prayed in faith; you cannot be assured that the person you are praying with is really in agreement, even if he says he is. You know where you stand, and they know where they stand—but only God knows if you have truly agreed in prayer.

You are accountable for yourself alone. You cannot be accountable for someone else, even if it is a spouse, a child, or another family member. Your faith will work for you, but it may not work for someone else. If you have stood in faith, trusted God, praised Him, and believed you received, you can do nothing else beyond that. If it appears your prayers have failed, there must have been something beyond your prayer. Quit blaming yourself!

Unfortunately, we often carry guilt in life for something that happened to another person. We may think that we have all the answers, yet we may never know in this lifetime what prevented our prayers from manifesting the results we expected. We cannot see into another person's heart—only God has that ability.

Many people need to forgive themselves for carrying guilt over someone else's life. Most often these feelings emerge when a loved one has died prematurely. We begin to question ourselves, *What more could I have done? What did I do wrong?* But when we examine our lives and realize that we did everything we could on behalf of another person's life, we need to leave it in God's hands. One day, in His timing, He will show us the answer.

Think about it. You know if you have bitterness in your heart. You know if you have unforgiveness in your heart. You know if you are standing in faith or if you have doubt and unbelief in your heart. If you have assurance that you acted according to God's

Word, you can relax and stop blaming yourself for the outcome of another person's life.

PAUL AND SILAS

> And at midnight Paul and Silas prayed, and sang praises unto God: and the prisoners heard them. And suddenly there was a great earthquake, so that the foundations of the prison were shaken: and immediately all the doors were opened, and every one's bands were loosed.
>
> *Acts 16:25-26, KJV*

Paul and Silas had been divinely led by God to the city of Philippi. Paul had a vision in the nighttime and as a result, sailed to Macedonia with other followers. The first place he and Silas arrived was Philippi and even though they were in God's will, they wound up in prison. Likewise, there are times when we're in God's will, but still face pressures, trials, and troubles.

How often have you thought, *I know I was in God's will, yet all hell broke loose?* I have learned over the years that tribulation comes for two reasons: either you are in God's will or you are out of God's will. Psalm 34:19 doesn't say that many are the afflictions of the sinners or many are the afflictions of the carnal Christian. It says that many are the afflictions of the righteous.

If you are in the midst of persecution today, it is important to understand that God will bring you through. "When the enemy comes in like a flood, the Spirit of the LORD will lift up a standard against him" (Isaiah 59:19), and that standard is the Word of God, which is the power of God.

Notice that Paul is in the will of God, yet he's in prison. The reason God gave Paul a vision in the nighttime to go to Macedonia was probably because He knew the tremendous tribulations Paul would face in Philippi. Paul obeyed God, but he and Silas found themselves in chains. I can only imagine Silas in the inner dungeon turning to Paul and saying, "Paul, run that vision by me again. Are you sure you had enough sleep that night? Are you sure you didn't just eat something bad the night before you had the vision? Are you sure we are in the will of God?" In reality, Paul and Silas knew they were in God's will, even though they had been put in prison. While in the will of God, trouble and persecution still came. "Yes, and all who desire to live godly in Christ Jesus will suffer persecution" (2 Timothy 3:12).

PAUL AND SILAS PRAYED AND SANG PRAISES

Acts 16:25 (KJV) says, "And at midnight Paul and Silas prayed." Notice, it says they *prayed*. What do you think they were praying? I think they were praying scriptures of deliverance, knowing God would deliver them from prison because they *knew* they were *in the will of God* being in Macedonia.

Verse 25 continues, "And at midnight Paul and Silas prayed, and sang praises unto God" (KJV). I believe the praises they sang were affirmations of their faith in God. I also believe singing— praise and worship—is the greatest expression of faith we can have. Prayer and supplication is to be made with thanksgiving and praise to God. We must enter His gates with thanksgiving and His courts with praise (Psalm 100:4).

Acts 16:25 says, "And at midnight Paul and Silas prayed, and sang praises unto God: and the prisoners heard them" (KJV). If the prisoners heard Paul and Silas praying to God and singing praises to Him, that tells us they were not being quiet about it. They were not praying and singing under their breath. Verse 26 continues, "And suddenly there was a great earthquake, so that the foundations of the prison were shaken: and immediately all the doors were opened, and every one's bands were loosed." As a result of Paul and Silas praying and singing praises to God, the prison doors suddenly flew open. The jailer and his family were all saved that night, and I would imagine that many of the prisoners were saved that night, also.

JOHN THE BAPTIST

And when John had heard in prison about the works of Christ, he sent two of his disciples and said to Him, "Are You the Coming One, or do we look for another?"

Jesus answered and said to them, "Go and tell John the things which you hear and see: *The* blind see and *the* lame walk; *the* lepers are cleansed and *the* deaf hear; *the* dead are raised up and *the* poor have the gospel preached to them. And blessed is he who is not offended because of Me."

Matthew 11:2-6

The John mentioned in this passage is John the Baptist. Like Paul and Silas, he too was in prison while in the will of God. When he was in prison, John heard about the works of Christ. Notice, Jesus told His disciples, "*Go and show John **again**.*"

I believe John the Baptist was becoming offended. He was probably thinking, *I am called by God. I was born supernaturally to two parents who were too old to bear children. I was anointed by the Holy Spirit in my mother's womb. I am the forerunner of the Messiah. Jesus wouldn't even have a ministry if it wasn't for me! I introduced Him. I was prophesied of by Isaiah. I'm the one whom Isaiah said would be the voice crying in the wilderness. What am I doing here in prison? Besides all this, I am the cousin of Jesus. Does that count for anything? My parents are close to Jesus' parents. Don't I deserve special treatment?* I think that John allowed the circumstances to offend him. Others had gone to prison and were delivered. Why not him?

In the midst of his imprisonment, John the Baptist began to doubt the ministry of Jesus, doubting that He is truly the Messiah. He was having questions and so he sent his disciples to Jesus. Jesus sent John's disciples back to him with His answer: "*The blind receive their sight, and the lame walk, the lepers are cleansed, and the deaf hear, the dead are raised up, and the poor have the gospel preached to them.*" I do not believe this was the answer John wanted to hear.

All of us have probably experienced moments in our Christian walk when we have held things that happened in our life against God. Most have probably carried animosity, offense, or bitterness at some point. In fact, there may be someone reading this book today who is offended at God because it looked like He didn't come through for you. You may even have said in your heart, *God,*

You've been faithful in the past but in this case You let me down. Perhaps you have even turned from Him because you know He is not supposed to let you down, but it seems like He has. Or it may be that you're not upset with God but you're upset with someone else. You may think, *My husband died and left me. Why didn't he stay? We stood together on God's Word in faith, but he just died!* You feel like you have been let down by a spouse or a friend because he or she should have stayed, but instead they died and left you here to fend for yourself.

I believe this is what happened with John the Baptist. He was offended at Jesus because things didn't work out like John thought they should. It is possible that John even compared himself to other people. When Jesus heard John's question, He responded, "Go back and tell John—**again**…the blind see, the deaf hear, the dead are raised. Go back and tell him." Jesus continued, "And blessed is the one who is not offended by me" (Matthew 11:6, ESV). What a powerful verse!

When you don't understand; when things don't seem to work out the way you thought they would; when you are confused and don't know what to do, don't allow yourself to become offended at God or His Word. Go back to what you've always known. Don't throw away what you know for what you don't know. Hang in there! God will explain it, even though it may seem confusing or contrary to His Word.

ELIJAH IN THE CAVE

When I read the account of John the Baptist questioning Jesus, it reminds me of the time Elijah began to question God in a cave.

> And there he went into a cave, and spent the night in that place; and behold, the word of the Lord *came* to him, and He said to him, "What are you doing here, Elijah?"
>
> So he said, "I have been very zealous for the LORD God of hosts; for the children of Israel have forsaken Your covenant, torn down Your altars, and killed Your prophets with the sword. I alone am left; and they seek to take my life."
>
> Then He said, "Go out, and stand on the mountain before the LORD." And behold, the LORD passed by, and a great and strong wind tore into the mountains and broke the rocks in pieces before the LORD, *but* the LORD *was* not in the wind; and after the wind an earthquake, *but* the LORD *was* not in the earthquake; and after the earthquake a fire, *but* the LORD *was* not in the fire; and after the fire a still small voice.

1 Kings 19:9-12

God brought Elijah out of the cave and told him to stand on the mountain. While Elijah stood there, a mighty wind came, then an earthquake, then a fire—but God was not in any of those. Finally, there was a still, small voice. The still, small voice was God saying, "Let's go back to how I've always led you. You don't need some special sign for this occasion." God was saying the same thing to

Elijah as He did to John the Baptist, when he had His disciples tell John, "The blind see. The deaf hear. Go back to what you know."

If you're in the midst of troubles and trials, quit seeking a sign from heaven and thinking, *If only four angels would come and tell me, if a bolt of lightning would come down from heaven, if a ball of fire would roll past me, I would certainly be convinced I'm in God's will.* When God isn't speaking, go back to what you know. Do not throw away what you know for what you do not know or understand. If you will simply trust God, even when you don't understand, God will eventually reveal the answers to the things you don't know.

WHEN THE BIBLE IS SILENT

The Bible doesn't explain why John the Baptist wasn't delivered, but that doesn't mean we dismiss this account from the Bible. We don't decide we're just going to give up on God because we don't understand why John died, even though he fulfilled the will of God. Sometimes the Bible is silent on why certain things did or did not happen, but that should not be an excuse for us to dismiss the ninety-nine percent of the Bible we do understand for the momentary thing we do not understand. We must always go back to what we know.

A number of years ago, we went through a lawsuit at the church I pastored. My wife, Loretta, and I prayed every day believing, *Today is the last day; today the lawsuit will end*—but it went on for three years! Every morning Loretta had scriptures for me to stand on. I sang those scriptures. I confessed them. My trust was in God, and every day we believed it was the last day of the trial. Daily we believed something would happen to end the thing, but it ultimately ended with a jury decision. Even though things ended greatly in our favor, we still had to endure it all the way to the end.

To this day, I still don't have all the answers as to why we had to go through that lawsuit. There were people in the congregation who quit the church over it. There were also staff members who quit because things didn't happen like they thought they should. The bottom line in that and every situation we face, is that we are not God. I refuse to back off from the Word of God—from the things of God—simply because I don't understand. God has *never* lied to me and He has *never* failed me.

Remember, Mark 4:22 says, "For there is nothing hidden which will not be revealed, nor has anything been kept secret but that it should come to light." I believe that God will reveal the answers at the right time. There are other things I still don't understand, but what do I do until the answers come? I return to what I already know. I cannot twist God's arm and force Him to give me an answer because I think I am something special and deserve an immediate response. I cannot control God. In the meantime, I will not hide my lamp under a bushel; I won't put it where others can't see it. I won't back off my testimony.

Why wasn't John the Baptist set free from prison? I don't know. The answer is not given in the Bible. John the Baptist wanted to know some of the same things we want to know: *Why am I here? Are you really the Messiah? Does Your Word really work? Do the promises of God really work?*

Instead of sending some great, special revelation from heaven, instead of sending angels to sing, "Glory to God in the highest," Jesus simply told John, "Go back to what you know." It was the same answer He gave Elijah, "Go back to the still, small voice. Go back to the Word of God. Go back to the signs and wonders still being performed."

DON'T COMPARE YOURSELF TO OTHERS

Isn't it funny how we are always comparing ourselves to each other? Don't do that. If John the Baptist had been able to see into the future and view the deliverance of Paul and Silas from prison, he would probably have thought, *Why them and not me?*

Jesus did not visit John in prison. Jesus just kept on doing what He was doing—healing the sick, raising the dead, opening blind eyes, opening deaf ears. John probably thought the same thing Jesus' disciples did when they were storm tossed at sea while Jesus soundly slept on the boat (Mark 4:35-41). The disciples thought, *Doesn't Jesus care?* In fact, they woke Jesus up and questioned Him, "Jesus, don't You care?"

Let's be honest. How often has that same thought come to you? Maybe you've never allowed those words to come out of your mouth, but in the midst of the storm—in the midst of the trial or tribulation—you've wondered, *Jesus, don't You care?* Don't you dare speak that thought! Stop before you utter those words because it is impossible for God not to care. He cares so much, and He will bring you the answer at the right time.

Jesus' answer to John the Baptist was, "Go and shew John **again** those things which ye do hear and see: The blind receive their sight, and the lame walk, the lepers are cleansed, and the deaf hear, the dead are raised up, and the poor have the gospel preached to them. And blessed is he, whosoever shall not be offended in me" (Matthew 11:4-6, KJV, emphasis added). In other words, He reminded John of what he already knew. When you don't understand, go back to what you know and don't compare yourself to others. Paul warned the people of his day to not compare themselves to others.

> We do not dare to classify or compare ourselves with some who commend themselves. When they measure themselves by themselves and compare themselves with themselves, they are not wise.
>
> *2 Corinthians 10:12, NIV*

Over the years, I've heard people say, "Well, I prayed for so and so, and he died. But she prayed for someone else and they lived. Why?" I don't know. I don't know all the thoughts and intents of their heart. I don't know what was going on in their mind. But I do know God is fair; He is no respecter of persons. What I don't know will get answered either in this life or in heaven, but God has promised me that He will give me an answer. And the same is true in your life.

As I mentioned earlier, one of the last things Jesus said before He left this earth was, "It is not for you to know the times or the seasons that the Father has fixed by His own authority" (Acts 1:7, ESV). When Jesus commanded His followers to go to the upper room and wait to be filled with the Holy Spirit, they questioned

Him about when He would establish His kingdom. Jesus basically answered, "That is not the issue. Go and wait in the upper room for the promised Holy Spirit."

Times and seasons are in God's hands alone. Answers are in God's hands and when His answers come, they are so simple that you will be thankful you didn't cast away your confidence. You'll be thankful you stayed with what you know. What you know has brought you this far, and what you know will take you to heaven.

WHAT ABOUT JOB?

What about Job and all the things that happened to him? When Job lost everything—including his children—when things seemed unexplainable, he didn't turn from God. Did he question God? Of course! Is it wrong to question God? No. But if you don't get an answer, don't throw the Christian life away. Be determined to keep following God.

> Then his (Job's) wife said to him, "Do you still hold fast your integrity? Curse God and die." But he said to her, "You speak as one of the foolish women would speak. Shall we receive good from God, and shall we not receive evil?" In all this Job did not sin with his lips.
>
> *Job 2:9-10, ESV*

Did Job understand everything that had happened to him? No. Even when Job's friends told him to give up on God, Job refused to do so. Job didn't even give up on God when his wife told him to *curse God and die.* It is possible you might someday find yourself in a situation so unexplainable that your friends advise you to just give up on God. If that happens, don't listen to their advice. Fall back on what you've always known. God will see you through!

In Job's life, God was on one side and Satan was on the other. God blessed Job's life; Satan cursed it. The first two chapters of Job tell us, before the story even begins, who was the answer and who was the problem. Yet, we often get that confused. Job's wife got it confused. Job's friends got it confused. They thought God was suddenly the problem. No, Satan has always been the problem, and still is the problem. But even though Job got confused, he never gave up on God. He kept examining his heart until he finally found the answer—and his life was blessed doubly at the end as a result.

Though He slay me, yet will I trust Him. Even so, I will defend my own ways before Him.

Job 13:15

And the LORD restored Job's losses when he prayed for his friends. Indeed the LORD gave Job twice as much as he had before.

Now the LORD blessed the latter days of Job more than his beginning; for he had fourteen thousand sheep, six thousand camels, one thousand yoke of oxen, and one thousand female donkeys. He also had seven sons and three daughters.

In all the land were found no women so beautiful as the daughters of Job; and their father gave them an inheritance among their brothers. After this Job lived one hundred and forty years, and saw his children and grandchildren for four generations. So Job died, old and full of days.

Job 42:10, 12-13, 15-17

Don't give up on God! There are double blessings coming your way! God cannot lie. His Word is true. He cannot bring cursing into your life; He can only bring good and blessing. God cannot bring sickness into your life; He brings deliverance and healing. Satan comes to kill, to steal, to destroy; he brings sickness and disease into your life. Don't give up on God! If you can't explain something, go back to what you know. God still leads by the still, small voice. He is still opening the eyes of the blind and the ears of the deaf, and raising the dead.

Job 13:15 says, "Though He slay me, yet will I trust Him. Even so, I will defend my own ways before Him." The word *defend* simply means, "I am going to stick with the Word and if God comes, I'll defend myself because I have stayed with His Word. Even if God slays me, I will trust Him." You may be thinking, *Will God slay me? Would He do that?* God is the giver of life; He will not slay you. What Job is saying in this verse is that even if God did something that appeared contrary to His Word, "I'll trust what I know. When I stand before God, I will repeat His Word back to Him." This is the type of stand we need to take in life, even if it appears that God has not stood by His Word. Go back to the truth you know: "Heaven and earth will pass away, but My words will by no means pass away" (Matthew 24:35, Mark 13:31, Luke 21:33).

I don't know where you are today. I don't know what has happened in your life. You may be at a place where you say in your heart, *I don't understand what has happened, but I don't want to completely quit coming to church. I'll come once in awhile, but when I'm not in church and living my life outside the church, I won't let people know I'm one of those Bible believing people. I won't let them know I believe when I pray I receive, because things have happened I don't understand.* I say join the club. Join John the Baptist. Join Elijah.

There are times in life when we don't know for sure why something has happened, but God has promised He will answer. He simply tells us to return to what we know. God is alive. People are being saved. People are being healed. People are getting delivered. God is not confused, even if we are at the moment.

Prayer:

Father, forgive me for wanting to hide my testimony and witness for Jesus Christ under a bushel. You promised one day You will explain the things I don't understand. You promised there is nothing secret that You will not bring to light. Father, I choose to rest in You and trust in You. You've always been faithful. You've never let me down. You've healed me, delivered me, brought finances into my life, settled my family, given me hope and eternal life. I'm not going to throw it all away for something I don't understand. I'm pulling my lamp back out and setting it on a hill, trusting that one day You'll answer what I don't understand. In Jesus' Name. **Amen.**

6

WHAT ABOUT JAMES?

People have often said, "I just wish I could have lived during Bible times; everyone was healed and everyone was delivered!" However, that is not true. The Bible is like our lives today. It is filled with stories of people who succeeded and also with stories of people who failed. For example, there are chapters in the Bible detailing the life of Solomon when he was "wonderful" and there are also chapters that tell of when he was "stupid." There are stories of Peter when he was "wonderful" and there are also stories of Peter when he was "stupid." People living during Bible times were just like us today.

Jesus chose everyday normal people. Think about it. How many times did Jesus say to His disciples, "Oh, ye of little faith"? How often did He upbraid them? "Upbraid" means He railed at them. In one passage, Jesus commended Peter, "Blessed are you for flesh and blood hasn't revealed this to you but my Father" (Matthew 16:17), then a few verses later He rebuked Peter and said, "Get thee behind me, Satan" (Matthew 16:23).

PETER DELIVERED FROM PRISON

And when he had seized him, he put him in prison, delivering him over to four squads of soldiers to guard him, intending after the Passover to bring him out to the people. So Peter was kept in prison, but earnest prayer for him was made to God by the church.

Now when Herod was about to bring him out, on that very night, Peter was sleeping between two soldiers, bound with two chains, and sentries before the door were guarding the prison. And behold, an angel of the Lord stood next to him, and a light shone in the cell. He struck Peter on the side and woke him, saying, "Get up quickly." And the chains fell of his hands. And the angel said to him, "Dress yourself and put on your sandals." And he did so. And he said to him, "Wrap your cloak around you and follow me." And he went out and followed him. He did not know that what was being done by the angel was real, but thought he was seeing a vision. When they had passed the first and second guard, they came to the iron gate leading into the city. It opened for them of its own accord, and they went out and went along one street, and immediately the angel left him.

Acts 12:4-10, ESV

Isn't this a great story? What always amazes me about this story is how Peter was able to sleep. Herod had just violently killed James, the brother of John, with a sword and had arrested Peter because the Jews were pleased with the killing of James. His intent was to also kill Peter (Acts 12:1-3). Yet, Peter slept bound by chains between two soldiers and with two soldiers outside his prison door guarding him, knowing he would probably be martyred the next day. I can tell you what I'd probably be doing in that situation. I'd probably have my eyes wide open, feverishly confessing, "*I believe I receive! I am the blessed of the Lord! I will live and not die!*" I most probably would not be sleeping!

Peter was at rest. He was resting in God's promises on the inside of him. The angel actually had to wake him up. Notice, what Peter could not do, the angel did for him. The chains fell off, the prison doors opened, and the gates opened. However, what Peter could do, the angel required him to do. The angel instructed Peter, "Put on your shoes and your cloak."

It is interesting that the cloak is mentioned because before Jesus went to heaven, He told Peter, "When you are old, you will stretch out your hands, and another will dress you and carry you where you do not want to go" (John 21:18). The phrase, "carry you where you do not want to go" is a reference to the manner of death Peter would suffer. When the angel told Peter to put on his coat, he was saying "It's not your time to die, Peter."

Peter thought he was dreaming. It wasn't until he walked outside and the angel suddenly disappeared, that Peter realized what had just happened. He had been supernaturally delivered from prison!

While all of this was happening, Jesus' followers were having a prayer meeting for Peter's deliverance. Their prayers were answered so quickly that when Peter knocked on the gate, they didn't think it was real. In fact, Dorcas answered Peter's knocking, ran inside to tell everyone their prayers had already been answered, and they argued with her, "No, that's not possible. We have barely begun to pray!"

Over the years there has been a belief that greater numbers of Christians praying increases the effectiveness of our prayers. But I don't believe this because the Word of God also declares, "I sought for **a man** among them, that should make up the hedge, and stand in the gap before me in the land, that I should not destroy it: but I found none" (Ezekiel 22:30, KJV, emphasis added). The number of people praying is not the issue; the issue is the amount of faith we have when we pray.

I'm sure believers were praying for James, just as they had been praying for Peter. What happened? Why wasn't James delivered? I am going to give you a very spiritual three-word answer. *I don't know.* This life is filled with "*I don't knows.*" James was part of "Peter, James and John," the trio that was so close to Jesus. I want to point out that even though the saints had probably been praying for James to be delivered, they didn't give up on God when he was killed. In spite of what had happened to James, they still gathered to pray for Peter.

Our lives are filled with both the blessings of God and things that might cause us to question God's faithfulness—things we don't understand and cannot explain. But regardless, we should rise up each day and declare, "This is the day the Lord has made. I'll rejoice and be glad in it! There may be situations in my life I don't understand but this I do understand, His Word is still true; it lives and abides forever! Heaven and earth will pass away, but His Word will remain forever!"

REASONS FOR UNANSWERED PRAYER

What are some possible reasons our prayers don't work? The Bible is filled with answers to this question. Here are a few possibilities. First, are you truly operating in faith? Only you and God know the answer to that question. Do you have unbelief in your heart? If so, get rid of it! Next, is there sin in your life? Psalm 66:18 says, "If I regard iniquity in my heart, the Lord will not hear me" (KJV).

Are you approaching God in fear? I have met people who needed surgery and told others they would believe God for healing, yet they were actually in fear about the surgery. You cannot trust God out of fear of going to a doctor. Faith is not built on the foundation of fear. Of course, if you have prayed and are in faith and choose to believe God rather than having surgery, that is completely different. Here is another question: Do you really want to be healed? Do you really want to live or do want to go on to be with the Lord?

Getting back to James, was James in faith about his deliverance, or did he want to go on to heaven? I don't know, and neither do you. The Bible doesn't give us the answer. This was something between James and God.

When a brother or sister dies whom we have known to be a man or woman of faith, we must return to the Word. What a sad thing it would be to one day get to heaven, learn the answer to your question about something that happened that you didn't understand, and discover you needlessly deserted God and spent many miserable years unnecessarily. During the times we don't understand, we must not forget all of His benefits (Psalm 103:2). God has loaded us with benefits. He has blessed us with benefits and the greatest of those benefits are not our possessions or our prosperity, but all the times God has never, ever failed us or let us down.

> Cast not away therefore your confidence, which hath great recompence of reward. For ye have need of patience that, after ye have done the will of God, ye might receive the promise.
>
> *Hebrews 10:35-36, KJV*

Confidence is different than faith. Confidence is built on experience. God has proven Himself over and over again. Each time He comes through, we have greater confidence He will come through the next time. When the Bible says, "Forget not all His benefits," it means to remember those times God has been faithful in the past.

Verse 36 says, "For ye have need of patience that, after ye have done the will of God, ye might receive the promise." There are times when we are tempted to throw away our confidence, especially when we don't understand. But God says, "Don't throw away your confidence because there is great reward. Keep following Me. Keep trusting and you'll eventually understand. You need to develop patience."

STEPHEN STONED

In Acts chapter 6, the followers of Jesus were multiplying. One time a dispute arose between the Greeks and the Hebrews. The disciples instructed the multitude of followers to select seven men from among them to deal with the day-to-day problems that occurred so the disciples could give themselves to prayer and study of the Word of God. Stephen was one of the seven chosen. Verse 5 says, "And they chose Stephen, a man full of faith and of the Holy Spirit."

> The number of disciples in Jerusalem continued to increase, and Stephen was being used by God to perform wonders and miracles among the people.
>
> Then the word of God spread, and the number of the disciples multiplied greatly in Jerusalem, and a great many of the priests were obedient to the faith. And Stephen, full of faith and power, did great wonders and signs among the people. Then there arose some from what is called the synagogue of the Freedmen (Cyrenians, Alexandrians, and those from Cilicia and Asia), disputing with Stephen. And they were not able to resist the wisdom and the Spirit by which he spoke. Then they secretly induced men to say, "We have heard him speak blasphemous words against Moses and God." And they stirred up the people, the elders, and the scribes; and they came upon him, seized him, and brought him to the council. They also set up false witnesses who said, "This man does not cease to speak blasphemous words against this holy place and the law; for we have heard him say that this Jesus of Nazareth will destroy this place and change the customs which Moses delivered to us." And all who sat in the council, looking steadfastly at him, saw his face as the face of an angel.

Acts 6:7-15

71

Acts chapter six reveals that in a short time, Stephen had become a great teacher of God's Word. In fact, when the high priest questioned him, Stephen began teaching about Abraham and went on to teach about Joseph, Moses, David, Solomon, and finally Jesus Christ, the Messiah. Chapter seven ends in the martyrdom of Stephen.

> When they heard these things they were cut to the heart, and they gnashed at him with their teeth. But he, being full of the Holy Spirit, gazed into heaven and saw the glory of God, and Jesus standing at the right hand of God, and said, "Look! I see the heavens opened and the Son of Man standing at the right hand of God!" Then they cried out with a loud voice, stopped their ears, and ran at him with one accord; and they cast him out of the city and stoned him. And the witnesses laid down their clothes at the feet of a young man named Saul. And they stoned Stephen as he was calling on God and saying, "Lord Jesus, receive my spirit." Then he knelt down and cried out with a loud voice, "Lord, do not charge them with this sin." And when he had said this, he fell asleep (died).
>
> *Acts 7:54-60, explanation added*

As Stephen preached to them, the power of God became so strong that those who were disputing him could not contend against him. They shut their ears to try to block out what Stephen was saying because he preached an outline from Old Testament times until the day in which they were living—showing that Abraham, David and the prophets all knew of the coming of the

Messiah, Jesus Christ. Stephen then accused them of persecuting and killing those who had foretold the coming of Jesus, and ultimately murdering Him on the cross. The people became so angry with Stephen when they heard the things he said that some stopped their ears while others grabbed rocks and began to stone him until He died.

PAUL'S STONING

Another similar incident happened to Paul in Acts chapter 14 while he was on his first missionary journey. He came to Lystra and was preaching the Word of God when a group of people stoned him.

> Then Jews from Antioch and Iconium came there; and having persuaded the multitudes, they stoned Paul and dragged him out of the city, supposing him to be dead. However, when the disciples gathered around him, he rose up and went into the city. And the next day he departed with Barnabas to Derbe.
>
> *Acts 14:19-20*

This passage says the Jews from Antioch and Iconium stoned Paul and they left him for dead. Can you imagine what those who had stoned Paul were thinking when they saw him back in town? He was probably cut, bruised, and bleeding. Yet here he was preaching the Word of God again!

Since Paul lived but Stephen died, we wonder, *Was Stephen in faith?* I personally believe that he was. Did Stephen have any unforgiveness in his heart? I don't believe he did because the presence of God was so strong on him that his face shined "as the face of an angel." Did Stephen really want to be delivered? I don't know. He had a glimpse of heaven and said, "I see Jesus standing at the Father's right hand."

Some people are holding grudges against a husband, wife or another loved one who left this earth prematurely to go to heaven. However, that loved one may have had a glimpse of heaven, they may have seen Jesus and decided to leave this earth. I believe very often we do not really know what has happened in a person's heart between him and Jesus, and we carry guilt. We think that we didn't pray enough, or we become angry because they went on.

Perhaps you have experienced this in your own life and thought, *How could they leave me? Didn't they realize how difficult it would be for me?* When this happens, you hide your testimony about Jesus, bury your lamp, cast away your confidence in Him, and turn away from following Him instead of continuing to live for Him. But remember Jesus said, "So do not throw away your confidence; it will be richly rewarded" (Hebrews 10:35 NIV).

If you have cast away your confidence in God, you need to make the decision today to quit living your life burdened by the fact that something happened that seemed contrary to the Word— something you didn't understand. Perhaps you have said in your heart, *My life with God stopped when he died...my life as a Christian stopped when she died...I haven't witnessed for the Lord or talked much about Him because my friend didn't get healed and I'm embarrassed to say I'm a Christian.* Why don't you choose today instead to say, "I admit that as smart as I am, I don't know everything; God does. One day I will know everything, but until that day, I'm just going to keep following God. I'm going to come back to what I know, and trust in His faithfulness. No longer will I hide my testimony under a bushel, but I will share about the goodness of God and all those times in the past that He has proven Himself faithful."

We have discussed what we should do when something happens in life that seems to contradict the Word of God, specifically when we have prayed on behalf of someone and it seems our prayers were not answered. We have looked at several examples from the Bible of those who were imprisoned because of their faith and lived to continue preaching the Word. We have also examined the lives of those who were imprisoned, but did not live. We discussed those who were stoned for their faith but died, and those who were stoned and lived. And we have come to the conclusion that even when we don't understand why things happen, we must not cast away our confidence in the Lord (Hebrews 10:35).

7

SEED NEVER FAILS

It is important to understand that the Bible was not written from the mind of man, but by the Holy Spirit of God. The Holy Spirit is not called the Holy "Mind" or the Holy "Brain"; He is called the Holy "Spirit," so why do we try to understand spiritual things with our man-sized brain?

Faith not only involves trusting God, but sometimes it also involves turning off those thoughts that come racing through our mind when we don't understand. When our mind says, *I don't understand this. This doesn't make sense*, that is when we need to say to our thoughts, "Just be quiet for awhile. You will understand one day. God is bigger than you!"

Thank God He has given us a brain. Over the years, however, I have met some Christians who seem to have turned off their brains. The Bible says we are to *renew* our mind, not *remove* it! God has not told us to cross the street by faith without looking both directions, nor did He tell us it's okay to text and drive and claim He will cover us with His protection.

CASTING DOWN IMAGINATIONS

> For though we walk in the flesh, we do not war after the flesh: (For the weapons of our warfare are not carnal, but mighty through God to the pulling down of strong holds;) Casting down imaginations, and every high thing that exalteth itself against the knowledge of God, and bringing into captivity every thought to the obedience of Christ.
>
> *2 Corinthians 10:3-5*

Paul warned us against wrestling inside—trying to figure things out in our natural mind. He said we are to *cast down imaginations*. Another word for *imaginations* is "reasonings." *Reasoning* is when we try to figure out why things happen in life that we do not understand. Of course, the first thing we need to do when things happen that we don't understand is look at the Word. Then if what happened seemingly contradicts the Word of God, like a premature death, we need to *cast down our reasonings*. We need to set them aside and simply walk in faith, trusting that God knows better than we do, and that one day we will understand.

Paul made a statement in 2 Timothy about leaving a companion behind who was sick. He made this statement without giving any further explanation—just like there was no explanation given about why James and John the Baptist went to prison and died.

Erastus stayed in Corinth, but Trophimus I have left in Miletus sick.

2 Timothy 4:20

Paul never explained why he left Trophimus sick in Miletus, nor did he say why his friend was sick. Did somebody pray for him? We have to assume they did. Did Paul himself pray for Trophimus? He probably did. Did Luke, who was also with him, try to treat him medically? Probably. Yet, some people read that verse and say, "See, healing doesn't always work."

The truth is that healing *always* works. Salvation *always* works. The Bible does not have to explain everything. There are some unknown things about what was going on in Trophimus' life. God, however, does not want us to focus on the unknown; He wants us to focus on the fact that healing is true.

If you are perfectly honest, you would probably admit you have a difficult time understanding the book of Revelation. Have you ever read through the book of Revelation—or even sections of it—and thought to yourself, *What in the world is this guy talking about?* If you had been given an actual glimpse of heaven and came back and tried to describe it to others, don't you think it would be difficult to explain?

Think about the book of Ezekiel. Ezekiel had a glimpse of heaven and tried his best, with his natural mind, to describe it. But heaven is beyond description. What I'm simply trying to say is there are times in life when God has an answer to your question that is far beyond what you can reason. Faith is not based on human reasoning; faith is based on the truth of God's Word and part of that truth is waiting on the Lord, knowing that things hidden will be revealed and things kept secret will be brought to light.

Have you laid awake at night wrestling with thoughts like, *Why didn't it seem like my prayer was answered? Why did I ask for something specific, but it didn't come to pass? I thought if I asked ANYTHING in Your name, (and I did Lord), it would be done?* You may have wrestled with these thoughts until you finally released the burden of trying to figure things out and said, "You know what, God? I can't handle this. I cast down these imaginations and cast the whole of my care on You because You CAN handle this!"

God wants us to stop wrestling and rest in Him. Walk in faith, do what God has asked you to do. Fall back on what you know. Don't throw away what you know!

THE FIERY FURNACE

King Nebuchadnezzar made a gold statue ninety feet tall and nine feet wide and set it up on the plain of Dura in the province of Babylon. Then he sent messages to the high officers, officials, governors, advisers, treasurers, judges, magistrates, and all the provincial officials to come to the dedication of the statue he had set up. So all these officials came and stood before the statue of King Nebuchadnezzar had set up. Then the herald shouted out, "People of all races and nations and languages, listen to the kings' command! When you hear the sound of the horn, flute, zither, lyre, harp, pipes, and other musical instruments, bow to the ground to worship King Nebuchadnezzar's gold statue.

Anyone who refuses to obey will immediately be thrown into a blazing furnace.

Daniel 3:1-6, NLT

After Nebuchadnezzar's decree was made, some astrologers went to the king to inform him that Shadrach, Meshach, and Abednego—whom the king had put in charge of the province of Babylon—had not bowed to the statue. They reminded King Nebuchadnezzar of his decree that anyone who refused to bow must be thrown into a blazing furnace. This infuriated the king, so he had Shadrach, Meshach and Abednego brought in for questioning.

Nebuchadnezzar said to them, "Is it true, Shadrach, Meshach, and Abednego, that you refuse to serve my gods or to worship the gold statue I have set up? I will give you one more chance to bow down and worship the statue I have made when you hear the sound of the musical instruments. But if you refuse, you will be thrown immediately into the blazing furnace. And then what god will be able to rescue you from my power?"

Shadrach, Meshach, and Abednego replied, "O Nebuchadnezzar, we do not need to defend ourselves before you. If we are thrown into the blazing furnace, the God whom we serve is able to save us. He will rescue us from your power. But even if He doesn't, we want to make it clear to you, Your Majesty, that we will never serve your gods or worship the gold statue you have set up."

Daniel 3:14-18, NLT

Some of us have set certain limits or thresholds in our lives. That is what Shadrach, Meshach, and Abednego were, in essence, doing. They said, "We don't believe we will be cast into the furnace. We believe God will deliver us from your decree and the furnace." They had a threshold in their thinking, but continued to basically say, "But even if this goes beyond what we have set as our limit or threshold, we will not bow down!"

Nebuchadnezzar was so furious with Shadrach, Meshach, and Abednego that his face became distorted with rage. He commanded that the furnace be heated seven times hotter than usual. Then he ordered some of the strongest men of his army to bind Shadrach, Meshach, and Abednego and throw them into the blazing furnace. So they tied them up and threw them into the furnace, fully dressed in their pants, turbans, robes, and other garments. And because the king, in his anger, had demanded such a hot fire in the furnace, the flames killed the soldiers as they threw the three men in. So Shadrach, Meshach, and Abednego, securely tied, fell into the roaring flames.

But suddenly, Nebuchadnezzar jumped up in amazement and exclaimed to his advisers, "Didn't we tie up three men and throw them into the furnace?"

"Yes, Your Majesty, we certainly did," they replied.

"Look!" Nebuchadnezzar shouted. "I see four men, unbound, walking around in the fire unharmed! And the fourth looks like a god (the Son of God-NKJV)."

Then Nebuchadnezzar came as close as he could to the door of the flaming furnace and shouted: "Shadrach, Meshach, and Abednego, servants of the Most High God, come out! Come here!"

So Shadrach, Meshach, and Abednego stepped out of the fire. Then the high officers, officials, governors, and advisors crowded around them and saw that the fire had not touched them. Not a hair on their heads was singed, and their clothing was not scorched. They didn't even smell of smoke!

Daniel 3:19-27, NLT

God will be with you in the fire, even if that fire is seven times hotter than normal! As I mentioned earlier, when we were confronted with a legal trial, every day Loretta and I believed God would deliver us. Every day we believed we would not have to go through the trial, yet we ended up in a three-year ordeal anyway. But guess Who was with us in the trial? The Fourth Man! In the things we didn't think we would have to face, the Fourth Man was there with us!

Shadrach, Meshach, and Abednego discovered something in the fire they never would have discovered if they had not gone through that experience. God did not throw them into the fire; evil, wicked people did. But God was there to help them, be with them, and bring them out. The men who threw them into the fire were consumed by the very fire that was meant to harm Shadrach, Meshach and Abednego. In other words, God turned the situation back on those who tried to bring them harm and destruction.

God's intention was not merely to take what the enemy intended for the destruction of Shadrach, Meshach, and Abednego and turn it around for them; His real intention was to deliver an entire nation, and He did!

Remember the story in Mark chapter 4 when Jesus fell asleep on the boat when the storm arose? The disciples thought, *Jesus is with us, so even if it looks like a storm is headed our way, surely we will not actually get into a storm.* But halfway across the lake, the raging storm they saw around them prompted them to wake Jesus and even question whether He cared about them because they thought they were going to die. Jesus was right there in the boat with them! You can know that Jesus is in the boat with you, just like He was the Fourth Man in the fire with Shadrach, Meshach and Abednego, and He will deliver you out of every circumstance!

DANIEL AND THE LION'S DEN

King Darius chose Daniel and two others to supervise the high officers and protect the king's interests. Due to Daniel's great ability, the king made plans to place him over the entire empire. The other officers, however, did not like this plan, so they tried to find fault with Daniel.

Then the other administrators and high officers began searching for some fault in the way Daniel was handling government affairs, but they couldn't find anything to criticize or condemn. He was faithful, always responsible, and completely trustworthy. So they concluded, "Our only chance of finding grounds for accusing Daniel will be in connection with the rules of his religion."

So the administrators and high officers went to the king and said, "Long live King Darius! We are all in agreement—we administrators, officials, high officers, advisers, and governors—that the king should make a law that will be strictly enforced. Give orders that for the next thirty days any person who prays to anyone, divine or human—except to you, Your Majesty—will be thrown into the den of lions. And now, Your Majesty, issue and sign this law so it cannot be changed, an official law of the Medes and Persians that cannot be revoked." So King Darius signed the law.

But when Daniel learned that the law had been signed, he went home and knelt down as usual in his upstairs room, with its windows open toward Jerusalem. He prayed three times a day, just as he had always done, giving thanks to his God. Then the officials went together to Daniel's house and found him praying and asking for God's help.

Daniel 6:4-11, NLT

Once they found Daniel praying, the officials went directly to King Darius to remind him of the law he had made and to accuse Daniel.

Then they told the king, "That man Daniel, one of the captives from Judah, is ignoring you and your law. He still prays to his God three times a day."

Hearing this, the king was deeply troubled, and he tried to think of a way to save Daniel. He spent the rest of the day looking for a way to get Daniel out of this predicament.

In the evening the men went together to the king and said, "Your Majesty, you know that according to the law of the Medes and the Persians, no law that the king signs can be changed."

So at last the king gave orders for Daniel to be arrested and thrown into the den of lions. The king said to him, "May your God, whom you serve so faithfully, rescue you."

A stone was brought and placed over the mouth of the den. The king sealed the stone with his own royal seal and the seals of his nobles, so that no one could rescue Daniel. Then the king returned to his palace and spent the night fasting. He refused his usual entertainment and couldn't sleep at all that night.

Very early the next morning, the king got up and hurried out to the lion's den. When he got there, he called out in anguish, "Daniel, servant of the living God! Was your God, whom you serve so faithfully, able to rescue you from the lions?"

Daniel answered, "Long live the king! My God sent his angel to shut the lions' mouths so that they would not hurt me, for I have been found innocent in his sight. And I have not wronged you, Your Majesty."

The king was overjoyed and ordered that Daniel be lifted from the den. Not a scratch was found on him, for he had trusted in his God.

Then the king gave orders to arrest the men who had maliciously accused Daniel. He had them thrown into the lions' den, along with their wives and children. The lions leaped on them and tore them apart before they even hit the floor to the den.

Then King Darius sent this message to the people of every race and nation and language throughout the world: "Peace and prosperity to you! I decree that everyone throughout my kingdom should tremble with fear before the God of Daniel. For He is the living God, and He will endure forever. His kingdom will never be destroyed, and His rule will never end. He rescues and saves His people; He performs miraculous signs and wonders in the heavens and on earth. He has rescued Daniel from the power of the lions."

So Daniel prospered during the reign of Darius and the reign of Cyrus the Persian.

Daniel 6:13-28, NLT

I can imagine as Daniel was praying after the law was enacted by the king, he probably thought, *I'll never be cast into the lion's den. God will preserve me.* Yet, he found himself thrown into the lion's den and not only that, but the cave was sealed with a large stone so there was no chance of escaping or being rescued by anyone.

WHY DID THIS HAPPEN

The lions in the cave were hungry and should have devoured Daniel, but God sent an angel to close the mouths of the lions. The next morning the king hurried to the lion's den and called out to Daniel. When Daniel answered, the king was overjoyed and ordered him to be lifted from the den. Then he cast Daniel's accusers in the den and before they ever hit the ground, the lions pounced on them and tore them apart.

Whoever digs a pit will fall into it, and he who rolls a stone will have it roll back on him.

Proverbs 26:27

It doesn't matter what traps the devil has set for you, God has a way of causing Satan to fall into his own traps. Hell was not prepared for and was never intended for people; it was prepared for the devil and one day, he is going to fall into it and will eventually be thrown into the lake of fire! Keep walking with God and watch Him deliver you out of the fire and just like Shadrach, Meshach, and Abednego, you won't even be scorched or smell of fire!

What Daniel's enemies intended for his destruction was turned back on them. That is the God we serve! He will turn the evil your enemies intend for you, back on them. Be patient. You may go through some fire, but you will not be burned. You may be thrown into the lion's den, but you will not be harmed.

Some of us need to remove all barriers and declare, "God, no matter what happens to me, I've never seen the righteous forsaken or His seed begging bread! You will not fail me! You will not forsake me! You are in the fire with me and will deliver me!" It simply comes back to this: *God is with you, no matter what you are experiencing in your life.*

THE SEED REMAINS THE SAME

Remember earlier when we were talking about the four types of ground in the parable of the sower?

Then He taught them many things by parables, and said to them in His teaching: "Listen! Behold, a sower went out to sow. And it happened, as he sowed, that some seed fell by the wayside; and the birds of the air came and devoured it. Some fell on stony ground, where it did not have much earth; and immediately it sprang up because it had no depth of earth. But when the sun was up it was scorched, and because it had no root it withered away. And some seed fell among thorns; and the thorns grew up and choked it, and it yielded no crop. But other seed fell on good ground and yielded a crop that sprang up, increased and produced: some thirtyfold, some sixty, and some a hundred."

And He said to them, "He who has ears to hear, let him hear!"

Mark 4:2-9

Even though each type of ground was different, they all had one thing in common—the seed that was sown into them. The first type of ground is hard ground, so when the seed is sown, it does not take root and is immediately stolen.

The second type of ground is stony ground, which has very little soil for roots to grow. The seed begins to produce but because it has no root, when the heat or the pressures of life come, it withers and dies. This type of ground represents the Christian who is not firmly grounded so when persecution and affliction come, he is offended and turns from God

The third type of ground is thorny ground. This type of ground receives the seed and has time to grow to the point where great blessings come into their life, but the deceitfulness of wealth enters in and they eventually turn from God.

The fourth type of ground produces crops thirty, sixty, and a hundredfold. The good ground represents the mature believer. How does it keep on producing? The key is this: "He who has ears to hear, let him hear" (Mark 4:9). The original Greek language carries the meaning that he who has ears to hear, *let him keep on hearing.* Why did one type of ground prosper while the others didn't? It heard longer. The good ground just keeps on hearing, therefore, it sees increases from thirty to sixty to one hundredfold. You would think by the time we get to be a hundredfold Christian, the devil couldn't pull anything over on us. But this is exactly when the enemy comes with his tactic to make us think that the Word doesn't work so we will turn from God. Don't fall for it!

If the only types of ground mentioned in this parable were the first three, we might think, *Well, I guess the seed doesn't always work. On the first type of ground, it didn't produce at all. On the second type of ground, the seed produced for a very short time. On the third type of ground, the seed produced a little bit longer but didn't last. Something must be wrong with the seed.* But the fourth type of ground is proof that the seed does produce. The good ground produced well and went on to produce thirty, sixty, and a hundredfold.

I want you to understand that *the seed ALWAYS works!* The ground is what makes a difference in what is produced. You may argue, "Yes, but my husband loved God. And my friend was so kind. They were such dedicated Christians." Unfortunately, the heart is the part of man you cannot see. The Bible says man looks on the outward appearance, but God looks on the heart (1 Samuel 16:7). As close as you may be to another person in your life, you cannot see into their heart; that is reserved for God.

When we have prayed for someone to be healed but they died, we must not doubt the healing power of God or that the Word is true when it says, "By His stripes we are healed" (Isaiah 53:5). We can doubt people, meaning we do not know what was in their heart or the conversations that took place between them and God, but we must not doubt God.

We cannot doubt salvation; the seed works for everybody. The seed represents everything it will produce. The seed will save you. The seed will heal you. The seed will prosper you. The seed will bless you. The seed will extend your life. The seed will bring great blessings into your life and keep the devil at bay. In other words, the seed never changes. In this parable, it is the ground that changed in every situation; the fourth type of ground convinces us of this. The seed has massive potential contained within it. If we'll deal with the sin in our life and truly trust God and pray in line with His Word, we will see the thirty, sixty, and hundredfold return manifested in our lives. When things go wrong in life, don't doubt the seed!

THE WORD REMAINS THE SAME

In the beginning was the Word, and the Word was with God, and the Word was God. He was in the beginning with God. All things were made through Him, and without Him nothing was made that was made. In Him was life, and the life was the light of men. And the light shines in the darkness, and the darkness did not comprehend it.

John 1:1-5

If the seed represents the Word, then we know the seed is Jesus, because Jesus *is* the Word.

Jesus remains the same. He never changes. His Word lives and abides forever!

Now He (Jesus) did not do many mighty works there because of their unbelief.

Matthew 13:58, explanation added

Where is the "there" that is mentioned in this verse? It is Nazareth, the city where Jesus was raised. Notice that Jesus did not do many mighty works in Nazareth because of their unbelief. In city after city after city, Jesus had done great things—healings, miracles, signs and wonders. However, in certain cities like Nazareth, He could do very little. It wasn't Jesus who changed from town to town; it was the ground—the hearts of the people—that changed. When Jesus arrived at His own hometown, He was hindered by the residents' unbelief.

THE MESSAGE REMAINS THE SAME

Woe to you, Chorazin! Woe to you, Bethsaida! For if the mighty works which were done in you had been done in Tyre and Sidon, they would have repented long ago in sackcloth and ashes.

Matthew 11:21

Jesus also mentioned Chorazin and Bethsaida, two cities He rebuked because of their legalism. Jesus said, "If I had done the same things in Tyre and Sidon that I have done here, they would have repented." The people of Chorazin and Bethsaida hated Tyre and Sidon. Why? Because they were such sinful cities. Yet, Jesus rebuked the two religious cities saying if He had taken the same message to the sinful cities, they would have received it.

Jesus preached in Nazareth. He also preached in Chorazin and Bethsaida. Jesus went from city to city, but *He did not change*. He preached from city to city, but *the message did not change*. He healed the sick from city to city, but *healing did not change*. He set people free from city to city, but *freedom did not change*. It was the people of each city Jesus entered that changed. No two cities were exactly the same because the people were different in each city. The people changed, but the Word never changed.

James and John the Baptist were not delivered, yet Peter, Paul and Silas were delivered. We don't understand this. We come to moments in our own lives that we don't understand and say, "I don't understand. Why wasn't my friend delivered? Why wasn't my husband delivered? Why wasn't my wife delivered?" But we need to realize that the hearts of people are no different than the different types of ground or the different heart attitudes Jesus found from city to city. These can change, but Jesus remains the same. We may think we know exactly what is in another person's heart—even those who are closest to us—but we don't.

THE WOMAN AT THE WELL

And he (Jesus) must needs go through Samaria.

John 4:4, KJV, explanation added

Why did Jesus "needs go through Samaria?" He went for one woman, a woman at a well.

Soon a Samaritan woman came to draw water, and Jesus said to her, "Please give me a drink." He was alone at the time because his disciples had gone into the village to buy some food.

The woman was surprised, for Jews refuse to have anything to do with Samaritans. She said to Jesus, "You are a Jew, and I am a Samaritan woman. Why are you asking me for a drink?"

Jesus replied, "If you only knew the gift God has for you and who you are speaking to, you would ask me, and I would give you living water."

"But sir, you don't have a rope or a bucket," she said, "and this well is very deep. Where would you get this living water? And besides, do you think you're greater than our ancestor Jacob, who gave us this well? How can you offer better water than he and his sons and his animals enjoyed?"

Jesus replied, "Anyone who drinks this water will soon become thirsty again. But those who drink the water I give will never be thirsty again. It becomes a fresh, bubbling spring within them, giving them eternal life."

John 4:7-14, NLT

Jesus gave the Samaritan woman the answer to eternal life. A little later, by the anointing of the Holy Spirit, He told her about her life, and she was suddenly changed in her heart.

The woman left her water jar beside the well and ran back to the village, telling everyone, "Come and see a man who told me everything I ever did! Could he possibly be the Messiah?" So the people came streaming from the village to see him.

John 4:28-30, NLT

After this woman's encounter with Jesus, her entire village was changed! Jesus was the same as He had been when He was in Chorazin and Bethsaida. He remained the same; the people who were receiving his message changed.

It all comes down to this: *Is your heart right before God?* If the answer is yes, then determine to keep it that way because you are in line for great miracles, signs and wonders. But keep in mind that you are not accountable for other people's lives. Of course we need to pray for others, but if their healing doesn't manifest, their salvation doesn't manifest, the restoration of their marriage doesn't manifest, we cannot allow their results to affect our faith. The seed never changes! The Word never changes! Jesus Christ never changes! He is the same yesterday, today, and forever!

HABAKKUK AND THE FIG TREES

Even though the fig trees have no blossoms, and there are no grapes on the vines; even though the olive crop fails, and the fields lie empty and barren; even though the flocks die in the fields, and the cattle barns are empty, yet I will rejoice in the LORD! I will be joyful in the God of my salvation!

Habakkuk 3:17-18, NLT

What kind of situation are you in now? You may say, "Well, you know the economy is really bad and it has affected my business. Maybe prosperity works sometimes and sometimes it doesn't." Wrong! Prosperity always works! You might say, "I guess faith works sometimes and sometimes it doesn't." Wrong! Faith always works! You may say, "My friend died. Maybe healing works sometimes and sometimes it doesn't." Wrong! Healing always works!

Notice, Habakkuk didn't throw away everything he knew because there was a famine in the land. You may wonder, *Why did he have to suffer through a famine? Wasn't he one of God's chosen?* Just notice that even though Habakkuk didn't understand, he continued to serve God.

You may say, "I'm in a fiery furnace." Well, the Fourth Man is in there with you. His name is Jesus and He will bring you out! Perhaps you feel that nothing seems to be working. Well, anyone who has ever served God has been right where you are. Don't give up on God because He has promised He will come through for you. He is faithful. He is dependable. If you don't have the answers you are seeking, remember He promised that those things that are hidden *will* be revealed. In other words, those things you don't understand right now *will* be brought to the light one day. Then you will understand and be glad you continued to follow the One Who is faithful, the One Who can be trusted, the One Who has the answers, the One Who has given us everything we will ever need in this lifetime!

MEET BOB YANDIAN

From 1980 to 2013, Bob Yandian was the pastor of Grace Church in his hometown of Tulsa, Oklahoma. After 33 years, he left the church to his son, Robb, with a strong and vibrant congregation. During those years, he raised up and sent out hundreds of ministers to churches and missions organizations in the United States and around the world. He has authored over thirty books and established a worldwide ministry to pastors and ministers.

He is widely acknowledged as one of the most knowledgeable Bible teachers of this generation. His practical insight and wisdom into the Word of God has helped countless people around the world to live successfully in every area of the daily Christian life.

Bob attended Southwestern College and is also a graduate of Trinity Bible College. He has served as both instructor and Dean of Instructors at Rhema Bible Training Center in Broken Arrow, Oklahoma.

Bob has traveled extensively throughout the United States and internationally, taking his powerful and easy to apply teachings that bring stability and hope to hungry hearts everywhere. He is called "a pastor to pastors."

Bob and his wife, Loretta, have been married for over forty years, are parents of two married children, and have five grandchildren. Bob and Loretta Yandian reside in Tulsa, Oklahoma.

CONTACT BOB YANDIAN MINISTRIES

Email:
bym@bobyandian.com

Phone:
(918) 250-2207

Mailing Address:
Bob Yandian Ministries
PO Box 55236
Tulsa, OK 74155

www.bobyandian.com

OTHER BOOKS BY BOB YANDIAN

Calling and Separation

Decently and in Order

Faith's Destination

From Just Enough to Overflowing

God's Word to Pastors

How Deep Are the Stripes?

Leadership Secrets of David the King

Morning Moments

One Flesh

Proverbs

Rising Out of the Pit

Spirit Controlled Life

The Bible and National Defense

Understanding End Times

Unlimited Partnership

What If the Best Is Yet to Come?

When God is Silent

From *A New Testament Commentary Series* (sold individually or as a set):

Acts

Colossians

Ephesians

Galatians

Hebrews

James

Philippians

Romans

PRAYER OF SALVATION

God loves you— no matter who you are, no matter what your past. God loves you so much that he gave his one and only begotten Son for you. The Bible tells us that "…whoever believes in him shall not perish but have eternal life" (John 3:16 NIV). Jesus laid down His life and rose again so that we could spend eternity with Him and experience His absolute best on earth. If you would like to receive Jesus into your life, say the following prayer out loud and mean it in your heart.

Heavenly Father, I come to you admitting that I am a sinner. Right now, I choose to turn away from sin, and I ask you to cleanse me of all unrighteousness. I believe that Your son, Jesus, died on the cross to take away my sins. I also believe that he rose again from the dead so that I might be forgiven of my sins and made righteous through faith in him. I call upon the name of Jesus Christ to be the Savior and Lord of my life. Jesus, I choose to follow You and ask that You fill me with the power of the Holy Spirit. I declare that, right now, I am a child of God. I am free from sin and full of the righteousness of God. I am saved in Jesus' name. Amen.

If you prayed this prayer to receive Jesus Christ as your Savior for the first time, please contact us to receive a free book:

www.harrisonhouse.com
Harrison House
PO Box 35035
Tulsa, Oklahoma 74153

The Harrison House Vision

Proclaiming the truth and the power

Of the Gospel of Jesus Christ

With excellence;

Challenging Christians to

Live victoriously,

Grow spiritually,

Know God intimately.

Fast. Easy.
Convenient.

For the latest Harrison House product information and author news, look no further than your computer. All the details on our powerful, life-changing products are just a click away. New releases, E-mail subscriptions, testimonies, monthly specials — find it all in one place. Visit harrisonhouse.com today!

harrisonhouse